'Quite a tour de force! Da[illegible] d to produce a thoughtful and [illegible] step advice and concrete examp[illegible] - and a must use - for any leader eager to position their business for success.'

Hubert Joly, President and Chief Executive Officer, Best Buy Co., Inc.

'Finally... a clear and comprehensive guide that sets out, step by step, how to create a compelling and actionable strategy. This book is a must read for anyone who needs to create a strategic plan and then execute it! The book gives straightforward and practical advice on how to think and act strategically. Best of all, it is written in plain English and not full of impenetrable business speak.'

Andy Ransom, Chief Executive Officer, Rentokil

'With strategy, timing is everything. This book is a reminder that strategic thinking is the first step to change management and success. It makes it clear that strategic thinking should not be daunting compared to the other day to day challenges we all face; it might even make those challenges easier! I love it, it helps me to clarify and structure my entrepreneurial ideas."

Eric Babolat, President and Chief Executive Officer, Babolat

'In a sea of very useful frameworks and great cases about strategy, what really strikes me is the lean testing methodology which is truly compelling. This is a great way to hedge uncertainty across cycles, geographies, business models and also personal biases. I really see a way to transform the strategic process into a learning process for my organisation.'

Aldo Bisio, Chief Executive Officer, Ariston Thermo

'I have been impressed by both the quality and practicality of the book. On one hand it is built as a guidebook that managers can use on an ad-hoc basis, particularly for large transformational initiatives. On the other hand, it reads fantastically well in one go, providing a holistic and fascinating view of what strategic thinking is about. The ideas and tools proposed in the book are definite success factors for all organisations.'

Nicolas Japy, Group Chief Operating Officer, Sodexo

'This book is an absolute must read for anyone who aims to successfully manage a business. Jerome and Davide have definitely succeeded in redefining strategic thinking, in a vibrant, thought-provoking and convincing manner. This book is really about the future of management.'

Albert Bourla, President & General Manager, Established Products Business Unit at Pfizer

'*How to Think Strategically* provides a simple and useful approach to the most misused word in business: strategy. Together with the app, it helps to focus on what is relevant.'

Daniel John Winteler, Chief Executive Officer, Miroglio Group

'How can you move from the simple desire to be strategic to actually having in place robust and clearly understood strategies? This book offers a practical roadmap to creating strategies, preparing an organisation for its implementation and building a framework that helps organisations embrace strategy as a true habit.'

Bernal Alejandro, Chief Executive Officer, Zoetis EMEA

'This is an enlightening book. Often while I was reading it I thought "Now I know why XYZ worked!" recalling in my mind situations and decisions I made in the past. It is a definite read for both young and seasoned executives. It is written in an easy, but at the same time, exciting style.'

Christina Miccoli, Chairman, CheBanca!

'Although strategic thinking and acting are definitely the most complex business processes, Jerome and Davide have brilliantly mastered this challenging topic and have created a book providing clear and direct guidance, not only on how to tackle these challenges but how to finish as a winner.'

Dr Andreas Penk, President of the Pfizer Oncology business in Europe and Country Lead for Pfizer Germany

'*How to Think Strategically* makes for fascinating reading on the three pillars of strategy: strategic thinking, strategy formulation and strategy execution. It is this focus on the three domains which make it unique, providing a holistic perspective to students and corporate executives. The authors need to be congratulated for writing the book in a simple and lucid style. I highly recommend this book as a must read for corporate executives as well as students.'

Dr P Singh, Director General, International Management Institute, Delhi, India

'This is a powerful book on strategic thinking. It is insightful, practically useful and provides a detailed roadmap to devising and executing a winning strategy.'

Reda Guiha, Director of the Specialty Care Business Unit, Pfizer France

'The authors are masters at integrating deep strategic thinking with wisdom and actionability. Clear, concise, effective, brillant!'

Gianemilio Osculati, CEO of Wealth Management at SanPaolo Assicura

'A reference book for anybody interested in strategy, including experienced executives eager to have an impact on their business.'

Sebastien Herzog, Chief Audit Executive, AXA Investment Managers

'A clever way to view and approach strategic management. Reminds us that strategic thinking is part of everyone's business.'

Gianpaolo Odarda, strategist at Ferrero International

How to Think Strategically

Your roadmap to innovation and results

Davide Sola and
Jerome Couturier

Harlow, England • London • New York • Boston • San Francisco • Toronto • Sydney • Auckland • Singapore • Hong Kong
Tokyo • Seoul • Taipei • New Delhi • Cape Town • São Paulo • Mexico City • Madrid • Amsterdam • Munich • Paris • Milan

PEARSON EDUCATION LIMITED
Edinburgh Gate
Harlow CM20 2JE
United Kingdom
Tel: +44 (0)1279 623623
Web: www.pearson.com/uk

First published 2014 (print and electronic)

ISBN: 978-0-273-78587-3 (print)
978-0-273-78884-3 (PDF)
978-0-273-78883-6 (ePub)

British Library Cataloguing-in-Publication Data
A catalogue record for the print edition is available from the British Library

Library of Congress Cataloging-in-Publication Data
Sola, Davide.
How to think strategically : your roadmap to innovation and results / Davide Sola and Jerome Couturier.
pages cm
Includes bibliographical references and index.
ISBN 978-0-273-78587-3 (print) -- ISBN 978-0-273-78884-3 (PDF) -- ISBN 978-0-273-78883-6 (ePub)
1. Strategic planning. 2. Creative ability in business. 3. Critical thinking.
4. Thought and thinking. I. Couturier, Jerome. II. Title.
HD30.28.S623 2013
658.4'012--dc23
2013026074

10 9 8 7 6 5 4 3 2 1
17 16 15 14 13

Text design by Sue Lamble
Cover design by Dan Mogford

Print edition typeset in 9/13pt Melior Com by 30
Print by Ashford Colour Press Ltd, Gosport

NOTE THAT ANY PAGE CROSS-REFERENCES REFER TO THE PRINT EDITION

To Stella, Lorenzo Alexander and Edoardo Maximillian, the true pillars of my life

To Paulina, Clarisse and Marie, for their infallible support

Contents

About the authors

Davide Sola is professor of Strategy and Management at ESCP Europe, the oldest business school in the world, and visiting faculty at AALTO Business School (Finland), IIM Bangalore (India) and Faculty of Economics Turin (Italy). He is also a Principal at 3H Partners, a firm dedicated to helping its clients to develop entrepreneurial solutions advising multinational organisations and governments in Europe, the USA and Africa.

Throughout his career, Professor Sola has encountered many strategic challenges which he has analysed and solved in many different capacities, as entrepreneur during the dotcom era, as executive in industrial groups and private equity firms, as corporate adviser at Mckinsey & Co., as economic adviser to governments and of course as scholar. This professional and intellectual journey has allowed him to develop unique insights into the process of strategic thinking which simultaneously marry the rigour of academic research and the relevance to business practioners. *How to Think Strategically* is very much the outcome of this journey.

Professor Sola holds a PhD in Enterprise Economics from the university of Turin, a masters in management, diplome grande école, and diplom kaufman from ESCP Europe. He speaks four languages (French, English, German and Italian) fluently. He lives in London with his wife Stella and his two sons Lorenzo Alexander and Edoardo Maximillian.

Jerome Couturier is a professor of strategy and management at ESCP Europe, based in London. He lectures in Business Strategy, International Management, Business Transformation and Innovation to EMBAs, Masters and in various executive programmes across Europe. Jerome is also a visiting professor at ESA in Beirut.

His work and research concentrate on enterprise and business transformation, sustainability of competitive advantage, international development strategies, strategy execution, and more generally on growth strategies. He is author of articles, policy papers, book chapters, case studies and academic papers presented at international management conferences.

Jerome is also co-founder and president of 3H Partners, an advisory firm dedicated to helping its clients to develop entrepreneurial solutions, supporting national and multinational organisations and governments in Europe, the USA and Africa. Jerome has accumulated 17 years of experience working in various industries such as healthcare, telecoms and media, automotive, and raw materials. He has been instrumental on a variety of topics from growth strategy, strategic positioning, and business model transformation, to entrepreneurship and strategy execution.

Prior to joining ESCP Europe and starting 3H Partners, Jerome worked with McKinsey and A.T. Kearney. He holds a PhD from diplom kaufman école normale supérieure, an MBA from Insead, and lives in London with his wife Paulina and his two daughters Clarisse and Marie.

Acknowledgements

No book emerges as the sole manifestation of its authors. Over the years many business clients, colleagues, scholars and students have strongly influenced and formed our thinking about strategy. Many people and circumstances have shaped the insights and experience we have gained and we owe an immense intellectual debt of gratitude to these people.

We are deeply indebted to Andrew Price for his editing support as well as his suggestions and contributions on how to make the content of the book more accessible and comprehensible.

Our sincere appreciation goes to all our colleagues at 3H Partners who have supported us in one way or another with data gathering, early reviews and many suggestions about content and cases. In particular Sandro Cuzzolin, Saurav Majumder, Angela Lo Pinto and Cristina Raiciu deserve special thanks.

Thank you also to the ESCP Europe Business School which has given us the best environment to cultivate our intellectual project. Our faculty colleagues have challenged us several times by suggesting major revisions. In particular we thank Giovanni Scarso Borioli for his energy and intellectual acumen which prompted us to implement fundamental structural changes that we are sure the reader will appreciate.

Clients and business partners have been great teachers in the development of our thinking around strategy, helping us to conceptualise their practices as well as by supplying us with plenty of examples. We are most grateful to them for sharing their time and experiences.

We would like to extend our appreciation to the Pearson team for their professionalism, encouragement and the immense support they have given us throughout the entire process. Richard Stagg recognised the potential for a new book on strategic thinking. Nicole Eggleton has been the best acquisitions editor we could have asked for, supportive and constructive in her feedback and always perceptive and tactful in her suggestions. Natasha Whelan and Linda Dhondy put the final touches in. And not forgetting Daniel Callaghan who introduced us to Pearson.

We are profoundly grateful to our friends and extended families for their patience, loyalty and generous encouragement for a project that took us away from them on several occasions.

Finally, there are our respective wives Stella and Paulina who have been pillars of support and understanding. Writing a book, we have discovered, is an all-consuming endeavour, taking over or overlaying all other concurrent activities. Without their encouragement, sacrifice, candid feedback and of course love, this project would never have seen the end.

Publisher's acknowledgements

We are grateful to the following for permission to reproduce copyright material:

Figures

Figure 2.2 from Sola, D., Couturier, J. and Scarso Borioli, G. 2013); Figure 4.3 adapted from *Diffusion of Innovations*, 5th ed., The Free Press (Everitt M. Rogers 1962) Copyright © 1995, 2003 by Everitt M. Rogers. Copyright © 1962, 1971, 1983 by the Free Press, all rights reserved, adapted with the permission of Simon & Schuster Publishing Group; Figure on page 74 from (Sola, D., Couturier, J. and Scarso Borioli, G. 2013); Figure 5.1 adapted from *Strategic Change and the Management Process*, John Wiley & Sons (Johnson, G. 1987) p.224, Figure 7.2, Copyright © Gerry Johnson 1987, with permission of John Wiley; Figure 6.4 adapted from *Competitive Strategy: Techniques for Analysing Industries and Competitors*, The Free Press (Michael E. Porter 1980) Copyright © 1980, 1998 by the Free Press, all rights reserved, adapted with the permission of Simon & Schuster Publishing Group; Figure 6.10 adapted from *Competitive Advantage: Creating and Sustaining Superior Performance*, The Free Press (Michael E. Porter 1985) Copyright © 1985, 1998 by Michael E. Porter, all rights reserved, adapted with the permission of Simon & Schuster Publishing Group; Figure 8.3 from *Blue Ocean Strategy: How to Create Uncontested Market Space and Make Competition Irrelevant*, Harvard Business Press (Chan, K.,W. and Mauborgne R. 2005) p. 5, October 2004. Copyright © 2005 by the Harvard Business School Publishing Corporation, all rights reserved, reprinted by permission of Harvard Business School Press; Figure 8.4 adapted from *The Alchemy of Growth: Practical Insights for Building the Enduring Enterprise*, Perseus Books Group (Baghai, M., Coley, S. and White D. 2000) Copyright © 2000, reprinted by permission of Basic Books, a member of the Perseus Books Group.

Tables

Table 6.2 adapted from *Understanding Michael Porter*, Harvard Business Review Press (Magretta, J. 2011) p. 41, Copyright © 2011 by the Harvard Business School Publishing Corporation, all rights reserved, reprinted by permission of Harvard Business School Press.

Text

Extract on page 86 from Sony Corporation.

In some instances we have been unable to trace the owners of copyright material, and we would appreciate any information that would enable us to do so.

Introduction

You are a born strategist. From an early age you have learned ways of doing things so that the benefit outweighs the effort. As a child you may have figured out how to get extra pocket money from your grandparents or how to come out on top in playground games. Later in life you may have pursued interests or nurtured relationships where the rewards you experienced were much greater than the time and effort you devoted to them. Trial and error will have led you to keep doing some things and to abandon others, favouring the behaviours which keep bringing rewards – a mark of a good strategy.

In our personal lives, when the reward exceeds the cost, we measure it in terms of happiness. In organisational life we might measure it in terms of the value created for shareholders or employees, or if the organisation is a charity or not-for-profit, the benefits for clients, patients or society at large. In each arena – personal or organisational – the strategist in us looks for ways to make the benefits outweigh the costs.

But while we are all born strategists, we are not always good at it. Look around and you will see people repeatedly behaving in ways that fail to deliver happiness and businesses ignoring the warning signs that indicate that a change in strategy is needed. Good strategists develop winning strategies time and time again. People and organisations who have mastered strategic thinking repeatedly extract disproportionately good outcomes from the resources at their disposal. Think of fellow students who got good marks despite not working as hard or seeming as gifted as others, or businesses that have similar resources and opportunities to their rivals but tend to outperform them on a regular basis. The chances are that this is the result of good strategy and strategic thinking.

Strategy making is an intuitive, mainly unconscious process. Think for a moment about your personal strategy or the strategy of your business. You would probably struggle to put it into words, even if you think you have one. This is because we do not develop strategy in a conscious, rational, linear way. Strategising is largely unconscious and relies heavily on intuition and, as a result, is efficient but not always effective. It is efficient in the sense that we can, most of the time, very quickly come up with a way of overcoming a problem or exploiting an opportunity. But although the process of intuitively generating a strategy may be quick, it is vulnerable to serious errors which can lead us to address the wrong problem or do it such a way that the costs far outweigh the benefits. These errors of judgement or unhelpful biases in our thinking could be caused by poor information or emotional pressure. Or it could be that we are acting on the basis of assumptions or ideas about people or the world in general that are flawed, but because they are so deeply embedded in our thinking we never question them. These mental shortcuts or routines save time and mental effort but, when they are inadequate or out of date, can lead to bad strategy.

This book will help you identify and avoid these normally unseen dangers and improve your ability to think strategically. It will take you through the whole process of strategic thinking and point out the skills, resources and type of environment needed for good strategy.

How to Think Strategically is more than just a book. Together with the app **(to download the app visit www.howtothinkstrategically.org)** that we have developed for you, it is a complete programme which will guide you on the journey from identifying an opportunity to creating value, right through to choosing the right activities and avoiding the wrong ones. We will help you understand what is possible and what is impossible and how to deal with risk. You will learn the importance of involving people in the strategic process so that the whole organisation understands and believes in the strategy. And finally we will challenge you to keep your strategy under review so that you can change course if you need to.

Who is this book for?

This book is aimed at everyone who wants to improve their strategic thinking in life or business. Managers and executives will discover practical ways to think and act strategically and to make strategy into a shared journey towards greater value rather than a glossy document that changes nothing. But students, parents, doctors and athletes will get just as much from this book as leaders in business, because the purpose of all strategy is to overcome obstacles in order to create value, whether value is defined as winning more races, raising great kids, getting top marks, helping more patients or bringing in more profit.

If you have no desire to see change in your organisational or personal life, or you are perfectly happy being told what to do by other people, this book probably is not for you. But if you want to see change and are willing to be part of making it happen, you will find in these pages the processes, concepts and tools that will channel your passion, energy and talents and turn them into results. Instead of being a mysterious and ill-defined process which happens in oak-panelled boardrooms, strategy will become a way of thinking and acting that, step by step, takes you towards your goals in life and in business.

If you see life as a purposeful journey into ever-richer experience where learning is lifelong and as natural as breathing, this book is for you.

Our core strategy beliefs

- **Strategy is everyone's business**. It is impossible for a few senior executives, even very gifted ones, to know everything that is important about what is going on in an organisation and its environment, and all the lessons that are being learned, not just in R&D, but right across the operation. They cannot know which innovations will disrupt the industry and which will disappear without trace and they rarely encounter customers on a face-to-face basis. Equally, it is hard for those who are close to the action, maybe in sales or production, to see the big picture. For this reason, strategic thinking needs to be happening all over the organisation and the strategic process needs to be inclusive and collaborative, drawing on the knowledge and know-how of the many, not just the few. The views of a smart salesperson on how to improve performance can be just as important as the ideas of a bright executive. Strategic thinking should not be seen as a discrete process owned by executives or the planning department, but as the natural way of working for anyone interested in creating value. Strategic thinking encompasses continuous learning and improvement, and depends on there being an environment where the exchange of information and ideas is encouraged.
- **Strategic thinking is both active thinking and thoughtful action**. Strategic thinking combines action and reflection to enable continuous learning. Interconnected global markets, fast-moving technologies and the lowering of barriers and restrictions in many areas means that challenges, solutions and opportunities are multiplying. The most successful managers will be the ones who can quickly work out what works and what does not. We therefore believe that a vital, indeed perhaps the most important component of strategic thinking, is coming up with ideas, testing them out on a small scale, learning the lessons and either rolling out or changing direction.

- **A free market for ideas.** We believe that market selection is normally a better mechanism for making decisions than assuming that the most senior person must have the best idea. But for this to happen, we must develop organisations free from the passivity, deference and silo thinking that so often characterise our hierarchical and over-controlled organisations. The strategic organisation is one where new ideas are welcomed and making mistakes is seen as essential to learning. In such organisations, everyone cares about performance and there is an open and well-informed dialogue on how the company and its various initiatives are doing. Staff in a strategic organisation have the freedom to vote with their feet as they choose to work on the projects that inspire them and with the colleagues who display leadership. They act like owners, always wanting to increase value and taking the initiative to make things better.

What equips us to write this book?

Search Amazon's business section under the keyword 'strategy' and you'll get more than 15,000 results. So why did we think we could add something of value to this vast literature? We have worked with a large number of organisations, in many countries and across several continents. We have helped managers in industries including telecommunications, automotive, pharmaceuticals, media and financial services to identify and overcome core challenges. We have worked with start-ups, family businesses, small- and medium-sized companies and huge multinational corporations. We have worked as strategy consultants with McKinsey, A. T. Kearney and 3H Partners and as professors with ESCP Europe.

Our roles as professors and consultants enable us to combine the best of what has been written with the emerging wisdom of those who actually practise the art and science of strategy.

Our work has given us a rare and valuable opportunity to not just observe but also to test out and evaluate different approaches to strategy.

Perhaps most importantly we have watched and listened; discussed, dialogued and debated over dinner, coffee and the boardroom table with CEOs and sales staff, entrepreneurs and investors, academics and practitioners, rising stars and elder statespeople; sat through time-outs, summits, brainstorms and crisis sessions; seen success and failure and thought long and hard about both.

We have brought together our learning from all of these sources and distilled it into this book. Every idea and every tool has been tested and refined against leading-edge thinking and real-world experience. Nothing here is superfluous or just the latest business fad, and we offer it to you with confidence.

Nevertheless, just as strategic thinking depends upon continual openness to learning, as authors we must declare that we want to refine our knowledge still further. So we invite you to contribute your own views and experiences to enable us to critique our work. As our understanding develops and our ideas are challenged or supported, we will use your comments to shape future versions of this book.

How to use this book

This book has two parts. Part one explains what it is to think strategically as an individual, highlights the factors that lead to success and goes on to explore the nature of strategy. Part two focuses on how you can put strategic thinking into practice in your organisation, taking you step-by-step through the process of devising and implementing a business strategy. We offer a number of practical tips and principles which will help make strategic thinking part of the culture.

There is an additional final part of the book called The Strategic Thinking Manifesto. To download this content, please visit **www.howtothinkstrategically.org**.

Because we want this book to be as practical as possible, we have included principles, tools and frameworks that you can use, and a wealth of case studies that illustrate how things work (or do not) in the real world. Most of us learn better when we are able to do as well as think. Each chapter ends with a summary of the main points and some things for you to think about and apply to your own situation.

We think that you will get more from the book if you read it, first of all, in chapter order. It follows a logical progression, with each chapter building on the previous one, so reading it in sequence will help you develop a solid understanding of strategic thinking. Once you have read it all, you can then refer back to particular sections as required.

The app

Over the years that we have been advising managers and executives, one question has been put to us more times than we can remember. 'We like the way you've helped us design and communicate our strategy,' they say, 'but do you have a tool we could use to take us through the whole process?' This is a fair question, given that we keep telling people that the strategy process must include certain steps and specific tools and frameworks, and we always felt bad that we did not have a satisfactory answer. Until now that is.

When we were writing the book we realised that an app would be an ideal accompaniment, helping to bridge the gap between theory and implementation. So we have designed the *StratPlanGenerator App* as a way of bringing the learning from the book to bear on your individual circumstances.

The goal of the app is to guide you through the process of designing a strategic plan. Of course, you still have to do the thinking, using your creative and analytical skills, but the app makes sure you are asking the right questions at the right time and provides tools and frameworks that will help. It forces you to think strategically but acts as a support and prompt and also takes away the hassle of producing the graphs, charts and slides. Think of it like a mountain guide or Sherpa; the journey to the top will always be hard work but you will have a guide to point you in the right direction and carry some of the bags.

If you follow the app right through, the end product is a presentation document that sets out your strategy clearly and logically in a style and language suited to senior management. But the app is modular and you can just use certain parts of it if you prefer. To our minds, the app is a godsend to any manager or executive who wants to work effectively and, therefore, needs to produce a strategic plan and revisit it as time and events unfold.

Finally

We hope you enjoy this book. The process of writing it was another chance for us to challenge our own thinking and refine our ideas, something we love doing. But more than this we hope that you will use the book to make a difference. Many of us sense that our businesses and our institutions, both private and public, require change or even radical transformation. Recent history, economic and social, tells us that many existing systems and established ways of doing things have long passed their expiry date. But even when the need for change is obvious it can be hard to know where and how to start. We offer this book to you as a guide and support.

Strategic know-how

Part 1 has two broad aims. The first is to examine what strategy is and how we can learn to think strategically in any context, not just in organisations. The second is to provide an overview of strategy in the business context and how it affects the health of an organisation.

Strategy has three main constituents: core challenges, coordinated, creative and sustainable actions, and value creation. The term 'strategy' is used and misused in a bewildering number of ways in a wide variety of contexts so we offer a clear and workable definition. We define strategy as a set of coordinated, creative and sustainable actions designed to overcome one or more core challenges in the pursuit of a higher purpose.

Strategic thinking is the process that enables us to devise practical actions that can overcome core challenges in the pursuit of a higher purpose. Strategic thinking makes extensive use of 'mental models' – the shortcuts and routines that our minds are constantly using to make sense of the world – and show that this has pitfalls as well as strengths. Strategic thinking transforms skills and motivation into increased productivity and should be applied when complexity and uncertainty are high and the risks and rewards considerable. This kind of thinking requires a mind and a thought process with some specific characteristics. The strategic thinking process is the series of steps which allows the strategic mind to perform at its best.

The effective strategic mind is aware of its own and other people's goals. It is able to see the likely impact of actions on people, structures and systems as they unfold over time, like the ripples that result from a stone being thrown into a pond. The strategic mind possesses a large repertoire of mental models and has developed expert intuition to enable it to use these models to rapidly identify issues, spot opportunities and propose a plan of action. It can also think creatively and imaginatively in order to produce innovative solutions. In addition to all of this, the strategic mind is able to monitor its own processes to spot biases and flaws and manage them.

Strategy in business is no different from any other type of strategy, although it has a language of its own. It has different levels and focuses, from corporate strategy to business unit strategy and functional strategy. For an organisation to be effective, its strategy must be fully aligned at every level.

Our main focus is on business unit strategy, which is about how to achieve a competitive advantage in each of the company's product or service markets. An organisation has a competitive advantage only when the outcome of its strategy, in terms of value creation, outperforms the average for its particular industry. Profit will be our proxy to measure value creation.

1 What is strategy?

MANY PEOPLE, EVEN IN BUSINESS, are very confused about what strategy really means. It is a word we use a lot to mean a wide variety of things, most of which have nothing to do with the real meaning. The casualty of this confusion is the quality of strategy in our organisations.

The word strategy is used in a variety of domains including business, personal or career development, politics and sport. Jerome recently heard the coach of a national football team saying: 'To win this championship, our strategy is to win all our matches one after the other.' This was not a great help to the team who already knew that winning matches was important. At a recent rally, a famous politician was asked about his strategy for the forthcoming election: 'My strategy is to spend my time in the field and listen to the citizens of this country!' Whilst winning matches and listening to voters are helpful things to do, neither constitutes a strategy. These examples of the misuse of the word are typical despite strategy being a key topic in universities and business schools around the world.

The word also means different things to different people. When we teach students or advise executives, we always start by asking the question 'What is your strategy?' Often, the answers are along the lines of: to grow, to be number one, to go international, to set clear objectives or to hit budget. While all these may be commendable, none of them are really a strategy. Strategy embraces all of these things: goals, objectives, planning, resources, and more, but it cannot be reduced to any one of them.

Perhaps this confusion is understandable given that there is no consensus even among academics, consultants or practitioners about what strategy actually is. London Business School Professor, Gary Hamel points out that 'anyone who claims to be a strategist should be intensely embarrassed by the fact that the strategy industry doesn't have a theory of strategy creation!'

Strategy has a long history. Much of what we are learning today is the application of principles used since ancient times, often in the context of warfare. In Sun Tzu's *Art of War*, we can read for instance that 'Ultimate excellence lies not in winning every battle but in defeating the enemy without ever fighting.' Born out of ancient China, strategy was also mastered by the Romans in both military and civil arenas. If we fast forward a few centuries, we see examples of Napoleon's strategic thinking that can be readily applied to modern business strategy.

What strategy is – and what it isn't

Since there is such confusion about strategy, we will first clear up some common misconceptions before we outline what strategy actually is.

Strategy is not:

One single element. Many eager strategists see vision as the key element of strategy. Strategy, of course, involves defining a vision or a strategic intention, but that is only a start. By the same token, strategy cannot be reduced just to a set of goals. Goals are essential but, to be of any use, they must take into account your starting point (i.e. your strengths, weaknesses, opportunities and threats) as well as the vision of the end state you wish to reach. Equally, strategy cannot be reduced to a thorough analysis of where you stand or to a list of things to do, important though these things are. A beautiful vision, a comprehensive set of goals or a masterly situation analysis will not, by itself, be enough. Strategy has to include all these elements: a long-term vision, a clear understanding of your current issues and opportunities, clear goals and a set of initiatives that will help you to achieve your goals and eventually reach your vision.

Having lots of goals. Companies frequently have either too many goals or the wrong goals. Strategy is about making choices. Having too many goals shows that you are unable to make choices. Remember, if everything is important, then nothing is important. Good strategies emphasise focus and trade-off over compromise. This enables the company to bring all its energy to bear on the right issues. But although focus and clarity are vital, the goals you focus on have to be the right ones. Goals can be wrong because they either do not address your key challenges, or simply because they are not realistic. Far too often goals are no more than wishful thinking. They state an ambition that is not grounded in reality.

A race to be the best. Strategy is not about beating others to be the first or the best. It is about being different, being yourself, being unique. Seeing strategy as a race assumes that the only way to win is to do the same thing but in a better way. In business, unlike sport, there can be more than one winner. Find something that you do well, that your customers value and that others cannot easily copy, and you have the essence of good strategy.

Having the perfect plan. Strategy is not about devising a plan and sticking to it whatever happens. The environment is in a permanent state of evolution, with opportunities and threats continually emerging and mutating. Your organisation is also constantly changing so that your strengths and weaknesses cannot be taken for granted. Adapting to change is therefore a critical component of strategy and the assumptions that underpin your plan should be relentlessly tested. Good leaders are constantly learning what works and what does not, and adjust their strategy accordingly.

Doing things. Strategy always involves action. But simply doing things without making sure that they will create value is not strategy. For something to create value there has to be a positive difference between the outcome of any action and the effort of performing it. And where there are several ways of creating value, the most advantageous must be chosen. Even if they belong to an organisation that is very good at doing a wide range of things, strategy makers need to select only those activities that will create most value.

Having ruled out what strategy is not, we can now begin to outline what it is. First and foremost, strategy should address the core challenges faced by the person or the organisation. And in order to establish what the core challenges are, a strategy must include a thorough review of the current situation both internally and externally. It should also state what will be done to tackle the challenges, spelling out specific actions. This implies focusing effort and resources on a few specific goals. This will entail making hard choices and trade-offs, setting aside some goals in favour of others. Well-crafted strategy should bring about long-term success, through creative actions that will be hard for others to copy.

Our one-line definition of strategy

Strategy is a set of coordinated, creative and sustainable actions (a plan) designed to overcome one or more core challenges that create value.

Strategy is built on the twin pillars of knowledge and uncertainty. On the one hand, there is situation analysis. This is an observation of current reality and contains much that we can be certain about because it can be observed and measured. This is our starting point, our point A. On the other hand we also have a destination and our plans for getting there. Unlike point A, this is hypothetical, because we cannot be 100% certain about the future and have to work on the basis of limited knowledge.

There are some things we can be fairly confident about but, as recent economic events have shown, there are always surprises in store. So inevitably our destination, our point B, and our plans to reach it must be built on the assumptions that point B will be better than point A and that our plans are the right ones. Here is the dichotomy of strategy; one of its pillars is grounded largely in knowledge, the other in assumption and hypothesis (albeit assumptions reached through careful reflection and analysis).

Only the implementation of the strategy will prove or disprove the hypothesis and therefore validate or invalidate the strategy. This is the essence of strategy. A strategy can only be considered to be good in the light of experience, once the hypotheses have been confirmed. We must also acknowledge that even point A, the analysis of the current situation, will sometimes contain a large element of hypothesis when we are in situations where we do not have the time or the resources for a thorough analysis.

If you work carefully through the chapters that follow, this book will help you to improve the quality of your hypotheses and reduce the element of risk, making strategy development less guesswork and more the result of a disciplined yet creative approach.

The key elements of strategy

Our definition of strategy is made up of three key elements. The first is the identification of the core challenges which represent the heart and soul of strategy. A strategy should be developed in order to overcome the one or more core challenges that prevent us from fulfilling a higher purpose. The second is a set of coordinated, creative and sustainable actions needed to achieve the aim of the strategy. Last, but not the least, is value creation – the necessary condition without which any strategy would be a waste.

Identifying the core challenges

Defining a core challenge starts with a clarification of what this higher purpose is. Stating the higher purpose, the ultimate goal, will make identifying the core challenges much more feasible, since it will enable us to identify the road blocks. Aim to describe something important and inspirational that will be a major part of shaping an individual's or an organisation's future. It should not be just a short-term operational goal.

A core challenge may be the root cause of many of the problems that block our progress or it may be the key that unlocks a massive opportunity. Resolving it will take the individual or organisation much closer to achieving their goals. Addressing core challenges is the exact opposite of fire fighting, a constant temptation for managers.

Unless we can identify the core challenges that face our business, we will always be in danger of treating symptoms and not causes. Take an example of how we could wrongly diagnose an issue and completely miss the core challenge.

A wrong diagnosis

Imagine there is conflict between two members of a management team. The CEO observes frustration, mistrust and argument. Coincidentally he also notices that several direct reports are not delivering on things that he expected them to do. The CEO diagnoses a personality clash between the two managers as the cause of the conflict and brings in an expensive consultant to coach and mediate. At the same time he also lets his direct reports know that he has noticed that their performance is below standard in several areas. He then sits back, pleased with his decisive action only to find that the problems resurface a few weeks later. The CEO then decides that much more assertive action is called for and he spends several hours making sure his team know how displeased he is.

> As he drives home, he reflects on how often it seems people can't get on with each other and don't deliver what is expected of them. What the CEO has failed to notice is that the two problems are related and that he himself is the main cause. Like many so-called personality clashes, the root of the problem is that neither person has a clear understanding of their respective roles and the limits of their responsibility. Both had been given the impression by the CEO that they were leading an important project. Instead of clarity, there was assumption and misunderstanding. Innocent actions and comments were interpreted as attempts to undermine or challenge and, as a result, resentment grew. The same lack of clarity on the part of the CEO explains why the direct reports did not deliver. Quite simply, they had never been told exactly what was expected of them. The root cause was unclear communication on the part of the CEO, but this was never addressed and, consequently, made the organisation weaker over time.

Core challenges have usually been around for a while. They do not just pop up suddenly out of nowhere. In some cases they have been around for so long that they are seen as inevitable. People just accept them or work around them. Solutions may have been developed but, if the challenge is still there, they obviously did not do the job. To avoid just generating yet more flawed solutions it is worth re-examining the challenge. We can make use of our creative mental ability to see the problem in a fresh way and open up new avenues of thinking. If all we do is to follow the same well-worn tracks that others have walked in search of a solution, then we are unlikely to find an innovative approach.

In the real world, core challenges are rarely well defined. They do not present themselves neatly packaged and labelled as core challenges. Indeed, what distinguishes great strategic thinkers is not so much their ability to solve challenges, but their ability to identify the right challenge in the first place. Peter Medawar (the celebrated scientist and Nobel prize winner) calls this the 'art of the soluble', where we identify the problems that offer the greatest rewards for our efforts because they are not too difficult but neither are they so simple that their solution is trivial.

Uncovering core challenges is not easy. The process starts by asking the question 'Where are we?' The answer can only be arrived at through an unbiased analysis of your strengths and weaknesses as well as a thorough study of the opportunities and threats in the external world. Such an analysis will produce many facts and observations, some quantitative and some qualitative, which will need to be classified and grouped in order to make sense of them. Through working with the data that we have collected, we are seeking to make links between the things we can observe and their hidden root causes. Among all the numbers, trends, feedback and surveys are the clues to the underlying issues that are holding back the business and the opportunities no one has yet spotted. Until we have correctly identified the root causes of what is going on within and around the company, we cannot name our core challenges.

Core challenges always involve uncertainty. Uncertainty about how the external environment will evolve and about the impact of our decisions. Uncertainty depends on perception. Perception is governed by our minds which, unfortunately, are subject to systematic errors, such as believing the level of uncertainty to be lower than it really is, or vice versa. One of the most common errors of judgement is to think that uncertainty increases in a smooth, linear fashion. Such a predictable progression would be nice but in reality it is fanciful. In most contexts one can only have a reasonable view of the future for a very limited period of time. After this time you are in the domain of guesswork, with a wide range of possible futures influenced by a multitude of variables, some of which may not even be visible as yet. Economic crashes, environmental disasters and terrorist attacks all have a habit of coming unannounced!

Identifying a core challenge also determines the goal of the strategy, which is simply the metric that measures whether or not the challenge has been overcome. A good and meaningful goal is just a proxy for overcoming the core challenge.

An example

Imagine that an organisation is running at 50% of its total production capacity and is just breaking even. A situation analysis reveals that if the company can reach 75% of capacity its costs will decrease by a quarter and it will be comfortably in profit, even if prices are reduced. It is clear from this that the core challenge is *to increase capacity utilisation by an additional 25%.* As a consequence, setting an objective of a 50% increase in sales is an excellent goal since it will indicate to everyone, at any point, how far the organisation is from overcoming the challenge. Achieving the goal means that the core challenge has been achieved. Conversely, increasing sales by 50% would be a terrible goal for an organisation already running at 80% capacity since, if achieved, it would overstretch the company, leading to delays and, ultimately, unhappy customers.

Coordinated, creative and sustainable actions

Actions are the visible part of the strategy. As humans, we use our bodies to achieve our aims. Similarly, actions are the body that achieves the strategy's aims. Actions should be selected because of their ability to address the core challenge you have identified. Actions that fail to do this are a waste of time and put the organisation in danger by diverting resources from the real challenge. This risk is often masked by our tendency to deal with issues that we already know how to deal with but that do not contribute to overcoming the core challenge. In a state of shock and panic following her first ever car accident, a colleague found herself trying to tidy up the debris from the road. She was unsure what to do, so she did something she knew about. In the novel *Animal Farm* by George Orwell the reaction of Boxer, the loyal farm horse, to every setback is to get up earlier and work harder – a tactic which leads to his eventual demise. We have seen a similar reaction in many organisations facing major challenges. They know that something must be done but, unsure of the way forward, they busy themselves with familiar tasks. Failing businesses tend to do what they have always done, only more so. Hence, when bureaucracies are in trouble, their response is normally to set up more committees. In such cases, we are avoiding the hard work of strategic thinking and salving our consciences by being busy. But the answer lies in working smarter, not harder.

The actions chosen should creatively exploit all existing resources and competences. Creativity is necessary since resources and competences are always limited. It is creativity that enables a great chef to produce an amazing meal from ingredients that are readily available to anyone. In the same way, creative actions combine or recombine resources and competences in new ways to overcome the core challenge.

Creativity in action

We once heard about a champagne company that was looking for ways to increase market share. It tried various methods but to no avail. In desperation it called in an expert in creative thinking. The expert gathered together the managers for a workshop, and started by asking them for words that best described the company and what it did. Their ideas were condensed down to a list of around 10 words and phrases, such as 'luxury products', 'memorable moments', 'sparkling wine' and 'made in France'.

The managers were then asked to repeat the exercise but this time without using any of the words on the list. They found this uncomfortable, as they were being asked to think in unfamiliar ways, beyond their normal mental routines. At first, they could find no other words, but as they were forced to ask themselves more searching questions about the company and its purpose, the ideas began to flow again. Eventually they reached

> agreement on the statement 'we are a firm dedicated to enabling successful celebrations'.
>
> Armed with this new, unconventional description they began to contribute ideas about how the company could achieve the growth it so badly wanted. The one which was adopted, with great success, was to attach to every bottle a booklet containing hints about making speeches. Because people are often anxious about making speeches at weddings and other special occasions, the booklet was an immediate hit. This simple, low-cost idea helped the company's champagne stand out from its competitors and an increase in market share quickly followed.
>
> This story shows the benefit of creative approaches which, although they may take us out of our mental comfort zone, can help us recognise and overcome the mental barriers that limit our thinking. Doing this requires courage, as colleagues will tend to be sceptical about anything which is slightly out of the ordinary.

Actions, as part of a strategy, should be coordinated so that they mutually reinforce one another. A strategy is always composed of more than one action, so the coordination of such actions is therefore vital. And the more sophisticated or complex the plan, the greater the need for coordination. Coordination also requires flexibility in that planned actions may be subject to unforeseen changes. Perhaps the outcomes achieved do not match the plans or maybe the business environment has shifted in a way that could not have been predicted. Even the most visionary and intuitive individual must accept that their plans will need to be flexed or even redrawn as circumstances alter and new insights are gained. Recognising when and how our plans have to change is part of the essence of strategy.

Actions must be sustainable. Sustainability is affected by how easily the actions can be implemented by the organisation but also by how easily competitors can replicate them. If the actions you have selected are easy for others to copy and adapt for their own means, it is highly likely that your strategy will have a very short-lived effect. The other aspect to take in consideration is the ease with which actions can be implemented. Far too often individuals and organisations devise strategies based on actions that make perfect sense from a theoretical point of view, but which are impossible to implement since they require resources and competences that the organisation does not have and cannot obtain.

Remember that the actions we select are, at best, a hypothesis about how the core challenge can be overcome. They are not written in stone and we should be prepared to discard or redesign them if it becomes clear that our assumptions were flawed.

Creating value

We have explored the heart, soul and body of strategy. But all of this only makes sense if it creates value. Value is one of the most ambiguous, multidimensional and subjective concepts in business. However, for the purposes of this book we define value as the positive difference between the outcome of any action and the effort of performing it.

Think about the choices you make in your everyday life, such as whether or not to go to the gym or whether it is time for you to sign up for a MBA. These judgements are made by comparing the benefits you expect to get with the effort or cost that would be entailed. In the case of the decision about signing up for a MBA, you would be comparing:

- the potential benefits associated with the higher status you will have, the higher salary you will be able to demand, and the knowledge and skills you will acquire (**the outcome**); with
- the university fees and the cost of books and travel, plus the long hours of study that will displace other, more pleasurable, activities (**the effort**).

If you do not think that the likely outcome of your action outweighs the effort required, then it would not make any sense for you to begin your MBA.

Value creation is therefore a necessary condition in selecting actions. But it is not enough to judge that the benefits outweigh the costs and that the action will create value. You must also consider whether there are other courses of action which would create even more value. Using the MBA example, there may be other options that would have even more of a beneficial effect, such as becoming an assistant to an important political figure or working closely with an internationally successful business leader.

The key messages of this chapter

- The term 'strategy' is used (and misused) when referring to different concepts – goals, objectives, planning, resources and so on – resulting in some confusion. The lack of a consensus on a definition contributes to this.
- We define strategy as 'a set of coordinated, creative and sustainable actions (a plan) designed to overcome one or more core challenges that create value'.
- The heart and soul of strategy is the identification of core challenges, i.e. the root causes. The identification of core challenges is not easy and starts with an analysis of 'where we are' in order to identify the causes to be treated (instead of the symptoms). Core challenges always involve uncertainty, or better 'perceived uncertainty', mainly linked to the external environment and to the impact of our decisions.
- The visible part of the strategy is represented by actions. Actions should be selected because of their ability to respond to the identified core challenges, should creatively leverage all existing resources and should mutually reinforce one another. They should also be flexible, able to

respond to unforeseen changes, and sustainable, meaning difficult to replicate by competitors but capable of being implemented by the organisation.

- The incontrovertible condition for any strategy is value creation, defined as the positive difference between the outcome of any action and the effort of performing it. Value creation however is not enough for a strategy to be chosen, since another would be preferred if it produces higher value.

ACTION POINTS

- Can you think of a story of amazing success? Reflect on the strategy that underpins this success. What actions were pursued to achieve such a success? Towards which higher purpose were they geared? What core challenges were successfully tackled?
- Take our one-line simple definition of strategy and apply it to your previous success story. You should see that it fits nicely. Strategy is not about complex definitions!
- Core challenges are the ones that get in the way of your higher purpose: what you would like to achieve, where do you see yourself in 10 years' time if everything goes well. Ask yourself whether you have a clear understanding of the core challenges you face in your personal or professional life.
- As an individual, do you feel that you create value in your day-to-day activities? Do the outcomes outweigh the efforts? Are your actions contributing to getting nearer to your higher purpose? Are they aligned and geared to solve one of your core challenges? If not, it might be time to challenge what you are doing!

2 What is strategic thinking?

THIS CHAPTER IS DEDICATED TO HOW WE THINK. In particular, how we can think strategically. Our strategies are shaped by our thoughts, and we cannot improve them without changing our thought processes. The following stories give a taster of strategic thinking in action.

An unexpected intuition

When Davide was working at McKinsey, he was asked to join an emergency project team to work with a major airline facing huge problems. The team established that the airline had only enough cash for the next 15–20 days, meaning that payments to staff and suppliers were at imminent risk. The senior consultant called a meeting to discuss the way forward. Around the table were industry experts, turnaround experts and consultants experienced across all aspects of business. We pulled out option after option, from route closures to special offers to price cuts, but when we studied them closely, none were fit for purpose as their impact would come too late for the beleaguered carrier.

The breakthrough, when it came, was both fascinating and unexpected. The senior consultant interrupted our discussion to announce that the correct action would be to increase prices by 20% from that evening, meaning that ticket sellers would charge more from tomorrow. The shocked silence that followed his announcement was eventually broken by my colleagues arguing that this was clearly the wrong thing to do. Their protests ranged from the fact that it had never been done before, to a prediction of customer revolt. Nevertheless, we eventually agreed that a price increase was a sensible, although unorthodox, way forward.

The result of the price rise was a sudden increase in revenue and cash in reserve, which gave the company sufficient breathing space to devise initiatives that would enable its long-term sustainability.

A fatal miss

From the mid-1990s until well into the 2000s, Nokia dominated the mobile phone industry. Its innovative, user-friendly handsets bettered those of more-established competitors such as Motorola and Philips. As technology developed, guided by a clear strategy of focusing on 'connecting people' (its tag line), Nokia managed to stay at the forefront: launching one of the first internet-enabled phones, entering the satellite navigation market and developing one of the first PDA operating systems (Symbian). In the mid-2000s Nokia was still the dominant player, despite increasingly stiff competition.

However in 2007, a highly anticipated announcement became reality with the release of the iPhone. When Steve Jobs had announced that Apple was entering the mobile phone market with a single device that also provided PDA/email services, online media, games and more, some saw this as another example of overselling by the Apple boss and did not take too much notice. But the market thought otherwise and around the globe eager customers queued to purchase the new product. The iPhone quickly became the phone everyone wanted.

Like the previous story, this account raises important questions about the thinking that shapes strategy. In this case, what were the executives at Nokia thinking, and how could they not see the 400lb gorilla about to enter the market? In short, how did they miss the iPhone?

In each story, the way people thought led to major strategic change. To understand how individuals, alone or in groups, can act in the ways described in these two stories, we need to explore some of the marvellous abilities and important limitations of our minds and thought processes.

What is thinking?

Thinking is the process which, in response to the need or demand for an action, engages our mind's faculties and resources in activities that generate a purposeful behaviour or action. The mind is formed by three connected processing systems:

- **perception** that allows us to transform the information received through the senses into impressions;
- **intuition** that makes judgements and decisions automatically and effortless; and
- the **reasoning** that we use when we consciously assess and analyse issues to arrive at a conclusion.

The process is always triggered by a **demand for action** (see Figure 2.1) where we are presented with the need for a purposeful behaviour. A demand for action might be one we generate for ourselves such as 'What do I want to do tonight?' or it might come from an external agent such as someone asking you whether you will commit to carry out a certain task. Note that an action or purposeful behaviour requires both a solution – the what and the how – and an intention to act. It is perfectly possible to have a solution to a problem but lack the intention to implement it.

The demand for action generates in our mind (the perception system) an **impression** of the problem we face. This is our view of the nature of the problem. The impression we form is influenced by emotional factors such as our current mood and our feelings about the issue as well as contextual elements such as the place we are in or the people we are with.

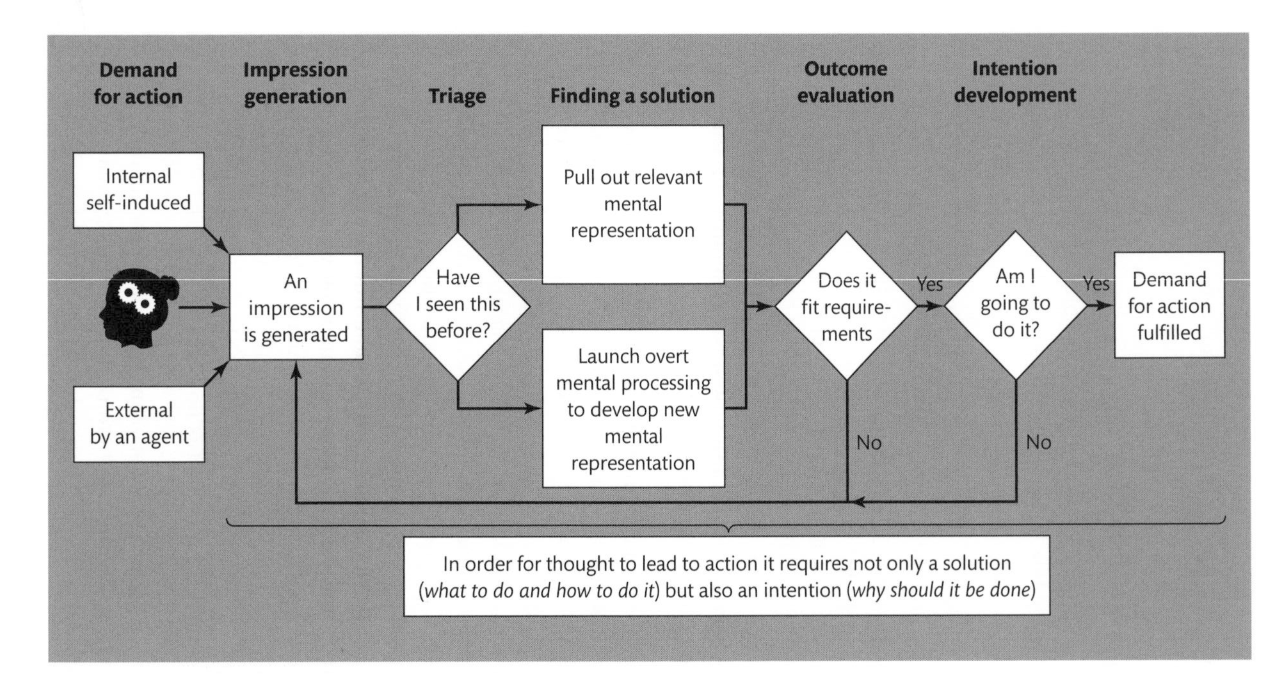

FIGURE 2.1 A simplified representation of the thinking process

At this stage in the thought process our reasoning system examines the problem, or more accurately our impression of the problem, to decide if the demand for action should be dealt with **by intuition** or **by consciously reasoning** it through. When we deal with the demand for action by using intuition, our mind looks through its collection or repertoire of **mental models** to see if any of them matches the problem in hand.

Mental models are mental representations of the world around us and how it works. Everyone has a collection of these models and we tend to use them without thinking to shape our actions because, to us, they are 'true'. They can be theories, concepts or rules of thumb that have become so deeply embedded that we are no longer conscious of using them. They can also be ways of behaving that we have become very skilled in, and which we frequently fall into using in order to manage situations.

These mental models are already present in our memory, so using them saves us the effort of consciously thinking through an issue from scratch. But if the model is flawed or we employ one that does not really fit the problem, we are very likely to experience failure because, being non-conscious, it is hard to evaluate them or make mid-course corrections. By and large we do not question our mental models, we just act on them. We treat them as 'givens' or things that can be taken for granted. But the complex, changing nature of reality means that what was a 'given' yesterday is a dangerous misapprehension today. Like generals who are perfectly equipped to fight the last war, managers' mental models can perfectly equip them for a business environment that is now history.

If there is a good match between the demand for action and the mental model, the mind pulls it from its memory and puts it forward as a suggested solution to the problem.

The good news is that most demands for action are dealt with in this way, effortlessly and automatically, as we have mental models to match most problems we encounter, as was the case in the airline story. The bad news is that using these ready-made solutions may lead to biases and errors of judgement when the solution does not really match the problem, as when Nokia failed to spot the implications of Apple's entry into the mobile phone market.

Our tendency to use minimum effort

A group of students from well-regarded universities were given the following problem to solve. A bat and a ball cost $1.10 in total. The bat costs $1 more than the ball. How much does the ball cost?

More than half of the group gave the answer as 10 cents. But a moment's reflection shows that the difference between $1.00 and 10 cents is only 90 cents and that, therefore, the answer must be 5 cents. The test was designed to measure people's ability to resist their first instinct, and most people, including highly intelligent people, tend to answer 10 cents because the sum $1.10 separates easily into $1 and 10 cents and because 10 cents seems about right.

The test illustrates the mind's tendency to use the minimum effort and to go with our initial, intuitive response without submitting it to scrutiny by our reasoning system.

Our tendency to simplify problems

An asset manager visits a company and falls in love with its products. The next day he starts to recommend the company's stock to his clients. The question his mind should be answering is 'Is this a good stock to recommend?' But answering this question involves looking at the future prospects of the company, the nature of its market, the quality if its management and, most importantly, whether its share price is undervalued.

> In the face of these demanding enquiries, his mind turns to a simpler question: 'Do I like the product?' and his affirmative answer to this question is used to answer the much more difficult question of 'Is this good stock to recommend?'

When we cannot find a mental model to match our impression of the problem we face, our mind will employ its reasoning system to generate a solution. Our attention then focuses on the problem and we are conscious of having to think about it. Our reasoning system scrutinises the problem, trying to reduce its complexity by breaking it down into a series of smaller, more manageable problems and then attempts to identify a solution. The likelihood of finding a solution is influenced by the mind's ability to use different types of intelligence (logical, mathematical, linguistic, etc.), blending together things and ideas from categories usually seen as separate. This may involve creatively 're-engineering' existing metal models, imagining completely new approaches or combining the two.

Take the story of the design of the 'ballbarrow', a wheelbarrow which, by virtue of having a balloon-like wheel, is less likely to sink into mud than conventional wheelbarrows. The inventor, James Dyson, borrowed the idea from the balloon tyres of amphibious vehicles. His creativity lay in seeing a use for a technology in a seemingly unrelated area. Creative thinking often involves abandoning the initial approach so as to encourage new and different ways of thinking. It seems that creative thinkers come up with these novel approaches not because they have more intelligence, education or experience, but because they think in a different way. They blend or even force together things and ideas from categories usually seen as separate.

As with intuition, the reasoning system is also prone to error, and when we concentrate our mind on a problem, we can risk investing a lot of energy in return for very poor results. There are plenty of situations where our focus on one set of issues can result in us ignoring important clues from other areas.

An important influencing factor in the choice of using intuition or reasoning is our level of emotional investment in the problem – literally how strongly we feel about it. The more our emotions are engaged, the more our mind will push the intuitive system to find a mental model that can be used to supply a solution. This can lead to errors of judgement when, under this pressure, an inappropriate mental model is selected for use. You can probably remember times when strong emotions, such as joy, relief, anger or anxiety, led to actions that, on reflection, may not have been the most wise as our powerful emotions 'hijack' our thought process.

Armed with a solution, developed either by intuition or by reasoning, your mind still has one more task to perform: deciding whether or not to perform the solution. This decision will be influenced by several factors including:

- how strongly you feel about the problem – your level of emotional investment;
- how capable you feel in implementing the solution successfully (self-efficacy);
- your levels of optimism or pessimism;
- your personality;
- whether the solution fits with your personal values and goals;
- whether the solution fits with the values, goals and culture of the people around you.

If these factors lead to a positive view of the solution, your mind is finally in a position to give the order to act. If not, it loops back to re-examine the issue or look for other solutions.

What is strategic thinking?

We start with a story that illustrates the real-world benefits of strategic thinking.

Strategic thinking in action

In 2006, we worked with the CEO of a leading animal health pharmaceutical company. During one of our first meetings he explained the main problems and opportunities facing the business:

- His industry was undergoing radical change as new distribution channels, such as online pharmacies and supermarkets, opened up, and valuable patents expired, making more room for generic products.
- The traditional role of the veterinary profession was under pressure as animal owners began to purchase drugs from other suppliers.
- He saw great opportunities in the increase in the number of animals being kept both for companionship and for meat and diary production, and the growing potential for improving the health and productivity of these animals.

His view was that all the problems and opportunities he had outlined could be resolved by overcoming just two core challenges:

1. Changing the focus of the company from being a provider of drugs to a provider of solutions.
2. Helping veterinary practices grow.

He went on to explain that his strategy, and the objectives of his top managers, would be centred on these two clear challenges. He was confident that all the usual corporate objectives, such as market share, would fall into place if these two core challenges were overcome. He told us about the actions he and his team had in mind and we were impressed by his realism as he acknowledged that some of these ideas may not work and that he needed to try them out, as inexpensively as possible, before any sort of corporate roll-out.

> Over the succeeding years a number of plans and actions were tested, modified and sometimes abandoned. But, throughout this time, the two core challenges and the actions taken to address them successfully guided the company through the process of adapting to a reshaped market. Today the company has reinforced its market leadership and positioned itself at the forefront of innovation. Its growth outpaces the market and most importantly its customers, the veterinary practices, have further increased their loyalty.

Strategic thinking is the ability to devise practical actions capable of overcoming core challenges in the pursuit of a higher purpose. And such thinking is not limited to the world of business.

Strategic thinking makes a huge contribution to productivity and performance. Experience, as well as research, tells us that teams or individuals differ enormously in productivity. Even when comparing people working in the same context, such as a competitive sports league or a single profession, top performers can be 10 or 20 times better than the least productive.

Differences in skill and motivation alone do not, we believe, account for these dramatic differences. Skills are essential but do not guarantee success. Many young footballers are signed by clubs on the basis of their skills but comparatively few progress to become champions. Equally, motivation is vital but not enough. Having staff who work hard and regularly burn the midnight oil will not, by itself, keep your company from bankruptcy.

Strategic thinking is the essential element that transforms skills and motivation into increased productivity. It is strategic thinking that identifies the right problem to solve, ignoring all the distractions, and therefore allows skills and motivation to be laser-focused and effective. All of this takes concentration and energy, and it would be both exhausting and unproductive to apply this level of thinking to the everyday problems we face such as what to eat or how to get to work. Strategic thinking is for when complexity and uncertainty are high and the risks and rewards are considerable.

What does it take to think strategically?

Strategic thinking harnesses the power of the **strategic mind**, using the **strategic thinking process**, to identify from a mass of data and feelings the right challenge to be solved, and then to generate a solution (see Figure 2.2). It also self-corrects; building in checks and balances to manage its inherent flaws. The strategic mind identifies challenges and develops

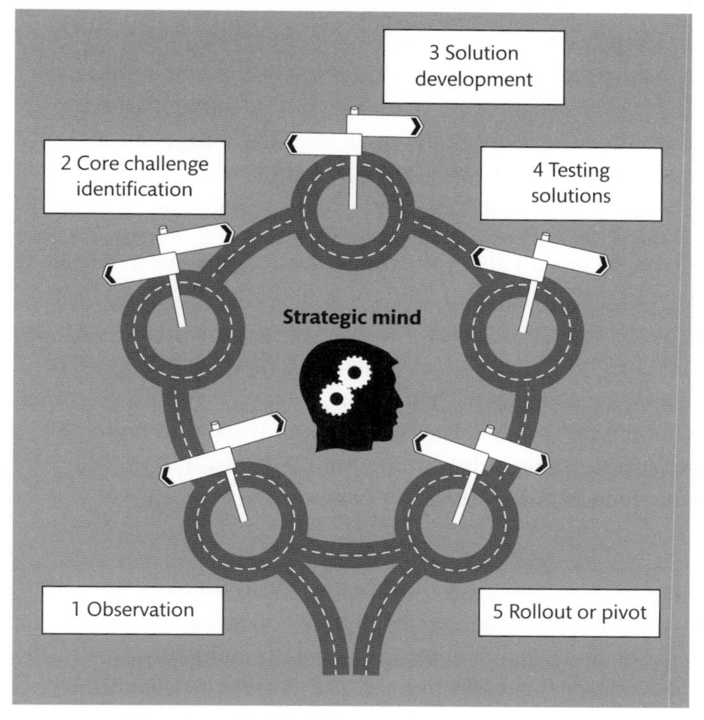

FIGURE 2.2 The strategic thinking process

Source: Sola, D., Couturier, J. and Scarso Borioli, G. 2013

solutions because every challenge overcome moves the strategic thinker closer to a higher purpose. This intrinsic motivation is the energy that fuels the mind to work through the different stages of the strategic thinking process.

The following features of the strategic mind are what makes it so effective.

The strategic mind

First, the strategic mind is **always clear about its own and other people's goals**. The strategic mind is not only capable of making explicit its own goals but also interpreting other people's. This is a particularly important feature of how the strategic mind works, as it enables every potential action to be measured against its own and other people's goals. Any course of action that does not bring a goal closer can be discarded or modified.

A second critical aspect of the strategic mind is **the ability to see an action in the context of time and systems**. An action never takes place in a vacuum and its impact may be felt long into the future, sometimes in unforeseen ways. Being able to visualise the impact of different courses of action and the reactions they may cause, both now and in the future, enables the strategic mind to avoid choices that seem to make sense here and now, but which may have disastrous consequences in other times and other places.

Another important feature of the strategic mind is **the possession of a large repertoire of mental models and the expert intuition needed to select the right ones**. We all have a wealth of these mental models so we also need well-developed expert intuition to correctly match models and problems. This ability is probably one of the most obvious signs of a strategic mind. People who have a strategic mind often have a reputation for being able to quickly spot issues and opportunities and, just as quickly, propose a plan of action.

The **ability to think creatively and imaginatively** allows the strategic mind to provide novel solutions, either by employing its faculties and resources to create a completely new idea, or by combining existing mental models in a new way. Strategic thinkers will borrow ideas from every possible source and join them together in creative ways to produce fresh solutions. They are not limited by conventional business thinking.

Two final features make the strategic mind unique. A strategic mind is **able to recognise and manage structural biases in its own thinking**. The strategic mind is more aware of its own processes. It is able to think about what it is thinking about. It carries out quality checks on its decisions and monitors the appropriateness of the mental models being used.

Strategic thinkers are not afraid of checking their thinking, and asking others to test out and scrutinise their ideas. This reflexivity (the ability to monitor and correct one's thinking in real time) depends to a great extent on the ability to understand and manage emotions. Our emotions determine our choice of mental models. The ability to be conscious of what we are feeling and, if necessary, moderate these emotions is a huge advantage in strategic thinking. This is the 'emotional intelligence' that Daniel Goleman, the psychologist, and others have written about.

Finally, a strategic mind is **able to work with other minds**. It is able to facilitate groups of people, possibly with very different views and perspectives, in such a way that creates synergy between individual thought processes.

The strategic thinking process

Having described the strategic mind, we now look in more detail at the strategic thinking process. This is the series of steps that allows the strategic mind to perform at its best to solve difficult problems or find a way of exploiting opportunities. This linking of mind and process is so fundamental that we often refer to the strategic thinking process as the strategic mind in action.

Observation

Observation may be direct or indirect. Direct observation is when we see or perceive something first hand. Indirect observation is when we organise or process our collection of first-hand observations to produce new insights. For instance, a glance at your sales results over the last two years will immediately tell you whether sales have increased or decreased. This is direct observation. But only further reflection and analysis will tell you that this is the result of just one or two valuable clients putting more business your way.

Observations carry with them impressions that may be positive or negative. Positive impressions might come from seeing that things are going well for us or from spotting an opportunity to do something new that will take us closer to the future we desire. Some years ago, Steve Jobs observed that 'people love to access all their music everywhere', that 'artists want to reach as many of their fans as possible', and that 'people are prepared to pay for design, simplicity and availability'. The positive impressions generated by observations like these led to the creation of the iPod, then the iPhone and the iPad.

Negative impressions are generated when we observe things that are not working or that are upsetting people; things that will make us unhappy if they are not solved. It was the impressions gained from their observations of the airline industry that led to Southwest airlines in the USA and Ryanair in Europe pioneering the low-cost airline model. They saw, for instance, that airfare prices seemed absurdly high and that there was plenty of capacity for additional flights but at smaller airports and at unconventional times of the day.

Sometimes our observations can trigger both negative and positive impressions. Consider the observations that brought us the Google Search engine. The negative impressions came from observations such as the poor quality of search facilities and the difficulty people encountered in finding the right information. The positive ones resulted from observing the exponential increase in internet use and the desire of businesses to reach their target audiences.

Identifying the core challenges

Defining a core challenge starts with clarifying the higher purpose we want to achieve. The core challenge is the thing that prevents us from reaching this aspiration. We must be careful, in stating our higher purpose, that we are describing something important and motivational that is a major part of shaping our future or the company's future. It cannot just be a short-term operational goal.

Our observations will identify many issues and problems that we could respond to. But strategic thinking depends on identifying core challenges. Remember the story about the CEO of the animal health pharmaceutical company? He could see a whole host of problems, issues and opportunities, but his strategic mind had distilled everything down to just two core challenges. He was then able to focus his company's efforts on those two pivotal areas, instead of dissipating effort by trying to do everything at once.

Thinking through these issues will enable the strategic mind to quickly evaluate whether it is worth pursuing a particular core challenge or if a different course of action would yield a better outcome. Indeed, one of the most distinctive traits of the strategic mind is not so much the ability to solve the most complex core challenges, but rather the ability to identify the 'solvable' ones.

Another very important benefit of defining a core challenge is that almost automatically you will be able to identify one or a few metrics that will enable you to check your progress towards the solution. Take again the example of the animal health company. It identified as its core challenges the need to change its focus from being a provider of drugs to a provider of solutions and helping veterinary practices grow. This enabled the company to have three simple metrics:

1. the increase of sales revenue from services rather than drugs;
2. the increase of the overall revenues of its veterinary clients; and
3. the correlation between 1 and 2.

Such simple metrics allowed the company to track its progress towards overcoming the core challenges and, more importantly, it provided individuals with feedback about the impact of their actions.

Solution development

Having defined the core challenge, the next step is to develop a simple, practical solution. We should not be seduced by sophistication. The ability to generate simple but effective solutions is both rare and valuable.

If a core challenge is worth solving, it is likely to involve some complexity. Complex problems have many intricately interrelated elements, meaning that changes to one element will have knock-on effects on the others. Just to make things more difficult, when we change or disturb one of the elements, the scale and nature of the impact on the other elements can be hard to predict. Anyone who follows financial markets will have seen this in action when anxieties amongst traders in one part of the world affects share prices in a different market on the other side of the world. This is different from problems that have many elements but which are not really interconnected.

Solving a strategic core challenge is usually a complex task, requiring a number of different steps. Often, each step involves a different set of related tasks, such as conceptualisation or experimentation, that in themselves consist of several discrete tasks. Therefore the first activity in tackling the solution of a core challenge is to reduce complexity. Trying to verbalise and visualise the different elements of the problem and the relationships between them will help us to understand the level of complexity as well as suggesting ways of reducing it.

The solution will always involve novelty. This might mean someone inventing something entirely new or creatively bringing together ideas or technologies that are already in existence, or a combination of both.

There are many ways of encouraging people to create novel solutions. Many useful approaches come from the work of Edward de Bono, the father of the lateral thinking movement. What most of these approaches have in common is that they force us to see the problem from a different angle or to think in a different way. (Those of you who want to know more should read De Bono's book, *Six Thinking Hats*.)

Other ways of getting people to think differently include asking them:

- to draw the problem using just images and no words;
- to brainstorm solutions, emphasising quantity rather than quality;
- to represent the problem using objects, or even to act it out;
- to imagine they have to explain the problem to an intelligent child who knows nothing about their industry.

Whatever technique you adopt, you will need to emphasise the importance of suspending judgement and banning criticism while the group generates ideas. The ability to critique and to point out risk is a valuable skill, but it can too easily overpower a great idea in its infancy. Also, as you will see later in this book, organisational culture plays a large part in whether new ideas are nursed to maturity or strangled at birth.

Testing solutions

In many cases, finding a solution to a core challenge will not be a single event but a process in which thinking is progressively tested and refined in pursuit of a correct solution. At each stage of the process, we have to make assumptions about what will happen, based on limited information. These assumptions or hypotheses are unavoidable. After all, we cannot finally know if something will work until we try it out. But we must treat them with caution. Therefore, it is important to tease out the assumptions and predictions that underlie any potential solution. We call this the **concept/idea statement**; a clear statement of the assumptions that the solution is based on and the outcomes which would indicate that the solution is correct.

Once we have clarified the concept/idea and its assumptions, we can move on to testing the merits of the solution. We call this phase **lean testing**, and its main focus is to find out if the assumptions we have made in reaching a solution will stand up in the real world. This process will produce important learning which will either help us with implementation or, if we decide the solution will not work, prove valuable in finding a better one. A solution should be tested as rigorously as possible in the environment where it will ultimately need to function. Simple prototypes should be constructed and tested to destruction to identify the limits of their performance.

It is important to use tests that are as real as possible because the human mind is prone to biases and self-delusion. So reality checks and testing are of paramount importance. They reduce the risk of failure and help to enrich and accelerate the learning process.

Tracking the outcome of each test will **validate the learning** – it will prove or disprove the assumptions that the solution was based upon. More importantly, the experimentation will provide, even in the case of negative outcomes, valuable insights about how to change the features of the solution to increase the likelihood of success. Like a scientist who learns from each failed experiment and does not give up, a strategic thinker should see every experiment as a source of additional insights that will assist in the search for the best solution.

Rollout or pivot

The knowledge gained from the lean testing should be enough to tell you whether you should proceed further with the solution or whether you need to 'pivot' – turn around and go back to the drawing board. If you are going to implement a solution, this will involve first the identification of what is needed for the implementation (i.e. financial resources, people, etc.) as well as the changes that will be required such as new processes, mental models or behaviours. If you leave this as an afterthought you will reduce your chances of success significantly. Identifying what needs to be changed and planning carefully so that new ways of working can be adopted quickly and smoothly is a definite enabler of successful solution implementation. Remember that a strategy can only prove its quality if it gets implemented. Excellent strategies that remain on paper are bad strategies!

Finally, rolling out a strategy requires a device to track its progress and impact. You need to carefully choose the targets and measures that will tell you whether or not things are going well. You also need to decide how the information, quantitative or qualitative, will be collected and what you will do with it.

If you decide to pivot, this is not failure. Even if it involves writing off some costs, the learning is invaluable – provided you use it! The next step then is to take your learning and feed it back into the process of finding a new potential solution.

The key messages of this chapter

- Thinking is the process which, in response to the need or demand for an action, engages the mind's faculties and resources in activities that generate a purposeful behaviour or action.
- Strategic thinking is the ability to devise practical actions capable of overcoming core challenges in the pursuit of a higher purpose. It is the essential element that transforms skills and motivation into increased productivity. It should be applied when complexity and uncertainty are high and the risks and rewards considerable.
- The strategic mind is able to cope with its biases. It possesses a large repertoire of mental models and has developed expert intuition – quickly spotting issues and opportunities and proposing a plan of action. It can think creatively and imaginatively and is able to recognise the structural biases present in its thinking and manage them effectively.
- The strategic thinking process is the series of steps that allows the strategic mind to perform at its best (see Figure 2.2).

ACTION POINTS

- Practise observation! Observe the world, look around you and beyond. Ask yourself what observations might affect you, your family, your financial position, your job, your organisation, your industry. Are these observations potential threats or opportunities to grab?
- From what you observe, try to investigate two or three core challenges in your personal life that are looming and preventing you from getting closer to your higher purpose. Ask yourself if you are missing anything obvious such as a fast-coming trend or event that might disrupt your life.
- As a strategic thinker, devise practical actions capable of overcoming your core challenges. Take into account biases! Once you have a solution ask yourself why it should be working but also try to discover why it should not. Then compare the two.
- Imagine how you could test the identified solutions, then through feedback adjust them or abandon them if necessary.

3

Turning strategic thinking into strategy

IF STRATEGY IS THE END POINT OR OUTCOME and the strategic mind is the engine needed to get us to that end point, the strategic thinking process is that engine in action. The question we address in this chapter is 'How do we engage the strategic mind in the strategic thinking process in order to produce an effective strategy?'

Engaging the mind in strategic thinking is not straightforward. It is not just a case of deciding to have a strategic thought. Rather it is like those times when a creative idea or breakthrough solution is needed but after lots of head scratching all you get is a blank sheet of paper. Sometimes it seems that the harder we think, the more elusive the answer becomes. In fact strategic thinking may well happen while we are away from the desk and engaged in activities that have no obvious connection with strategy. A walk in the countryside, reading a book or just daydreaming may provide a more fruitful context for strategic thinking than sitting in the office. Like Archimedes who had his Eureka moment in the bathtub, answers sometime come in unexpected places.

At times like this, it may seem as though the thought has come from nowhere, but this is a misconception. Strategic thinking is an additive process, in which our minds are constantly gathering knowledge of all types and making associations – connecting the dots – between new and existing information. These associations, sometimes between seemingly unrelated pieces of information, can generate fresh insights and enable us to make sense of previously intractable issues. This process can continue even when our conscious mind is focused elsewhere. In moments of reflection these insights then rise to the level of consciousness.

Frederick Kekulé's discovery of the structure of Benzene was critical to the development of modern organic chemistry, but it did not happen in the laboratory. It came when he was gazing at the flames of his fire and the shapes of the flames triggered a new insight. Although it seems like a sudden epiphany, such a breakthrough usually comes when we have been working on a problem. Although our conscious focus may have been on another issue, our minds are still working. Strategic thought can be enabled by making sure the right conditions are in place:

1. freedom to explore and discuss new and challenging ideas;
2. the availability of time and resources to think and act creatively;
3. a willingness on the part of the person to both learn and unlearn; to be ready to ditch old ways of thinking as well as adopting new ones.

These conditions are not always present in corporate settings, where factors including politics, history and the desire to fit in promote thinking that tends to be incremental and unadventurous. But while it might be difficult to create the right conditions in an organisational setting, it is not impossible. And, as the following example shows, learning, the main enabler of strategic thinking, is vital.

Jeff Bezos - strategic thinking using narrative

Amazon's Jeff Bezos is the quintessential strategic thinker, able to use both analysis and intuition and recognising the need for both approaches. According to Jeff, 'For every leader in the company, not just for me, there are decisions that can be made by analysis. The great thing about fact-based (analytical) decisions is that they overrule the hierarchy. The most junior person in the company can win an argument with the most senior person with a fact-based decision. Unfortunately, there's this whole other set of decisions that you can't ultimately boil down to a logical fact-based problem solving approach.' For this latter type of decision, Jeff relies on judgement.

Regardless of whether the decision was made with analysis or intuition, Jeff has a novel way of making sure it is well grounded in strategic thought. Before ideas or proposals can be discussed, they have to be expressed not in bullet points, but in a written document that sets out the issue and the author's thinking about what could be done and why. Jeff calls these narratives, and uses them to make sure he and his managers have thought through their arguments carefully.

Developing an argument in whole sentences forces managers to make explicit the assumptions, arguments and choices that guide their thinking. These narratives are then read carefully - in silence - at the meeting before they are discussed, allowing the readers to immerse themselves in the author's thinking. This process encourages a depth of reflection and clarity of thought that would not happen with a quick PowerPoint presentation and a time-pressured discussion.

The link between learning and strategic thinking

Strategic thinking is a process of continuous learning. From observation to the identification of the core challenge, from solution development and testing to deciding to implement the solution or to abandon, learning is the key enabler of strategic thinking. The learning process is not always steady and linear, instead it is full of loops, spirals and changes in direction as we wrestle with strategic questions such as why we need to change, how we need to change and what we need to change into.

Humans are, by nature, learners. Our curiosity drives us to seek out learning in innumerable ways. We watch, we ask questions, we read, we listen, we feel, we think and we experience. Books, online information, images, places and sounds all provide the raw material for learning. And although we create special places for learning – schools and colleges – most learning happens as we deal with the challenges of everyday living.

Learning is the process of transforming experience into purposeful action. Our experiences – our interactions with our environment – supply the raw material of learning. But until the raw material is processed into action, no learning has taken place. Reg Revans, the father of action learning, expressed this well when he said that 'there can be no learning without action and no (sober and deliberate) action without learning'. Although we talk about learning from experience, experience by itself is worth nothing until it results in a change in our knowledge, skills or mind-set. But the amount of effort and impact associated with learning in these three areas is very different.

Learning knowledge such as facts or figures can be done easily and with little effort, but the impact of such learning is normally limited. We may soon forget what we have learned. Think about the exams you revised for in school. Historical dates, mathematical formulae and quotes from great literature were learned by rote but a few months after the exam, most had been forgotten. The impact on your life was minimal.

Learning a skill requires more effort. There may be a knowledge component, but even when this has been learned, practice is required before you could be said to have learned the skill. Take learning to drive a car. There are facts involved, but these can be assimilated without ever getting behind the wheel of a car. Learning the skill of driving entails trial and error, careful practice and feedback from someone more skilled. But once learned, this skill is not easily forgotten. Like learning to swim or to ride a bike, the skill can be retained for a lifetime.

But if learning a skill can be difficult, **learning to change a mind-set** is even more challenging. Our mind-sets, or mental models, are the principles which shape our thoughts and actions. These are the biases, assumptions, preferences and prejudices which we have somehow accumulated over the years. Our mind-sets are so deeply embedded that, by and large, we are unaware of what they are and how they got there. They are not the result of conscious reasoning; instead they have been absorbed from our experience. Education, family, role models and national culture may all play a part in shaping our mind-sets.

Mind-sets vary according to context. We may act differently at work than we do at home, with different ideas of what is acceptable depending on where we are. In teams and organisations, mind-sets can develop and spread rapidly.

If you think about organisations you have worked in, you will probably recognise that norms of behaviour or ways of making decisions which have their roots in the past can persist for many years even when they are no longer helpful. When a new manager tries to introduce change, the old ways can be remarkably resilient.

It is the deeply-rooted nature of mind-sets which makes them hard to change. Acquiring new facts and learning skills requires effort, but learning new mind-sets requires us to reconsider or relinquish basic beliefs and values. In many cases, people prefer to stick with what they know even when there is a strong rational case for change. It is this tendency to hold on to the familiar at all costs, and the problems this causes, that led Tom Peters, the management thinker, to mischievously suggest that organisations should forget learning and learn forgetting. Changing mind-sets requires an openness of mind and a willingness to challenge fondly held beliefs. It requires humility, in that we might have to admit that we have been wrong. These sorts of qualities – openness to challenge and humility – are not found in abundance in top management, but the rewards are considerable.

True innovation and breakthrough thinking depend on being ready to change our thinking about how things work. Seeing and seizing new opportunities demands new thinking. Managers who recognise that they may need to change their mind-sets stand a much better chance of adapting to the ever-increasing speed of business change than those who expend all their energy in defending the status quo.

How to maximise strategic learning

If learning is the enabler of strategic thinking, what can we do to support and enable learning? We create opportunities for learning when we ask questions, when we observe what goes on around us, when we experiment with new ways of doing things and when we challenge our mind-sets. But these things are just part of the learning process, they are triggers for learning. For learning to happen, we also need to have the ability to reflect. And we need to be in an environment that facilitates learning, or at least one that does not constrain it too much. Figure 3.1 illustrates these requirements. It shows the strategic mind in the centre of the strategy process. Around the mind are factors that can trigger learning

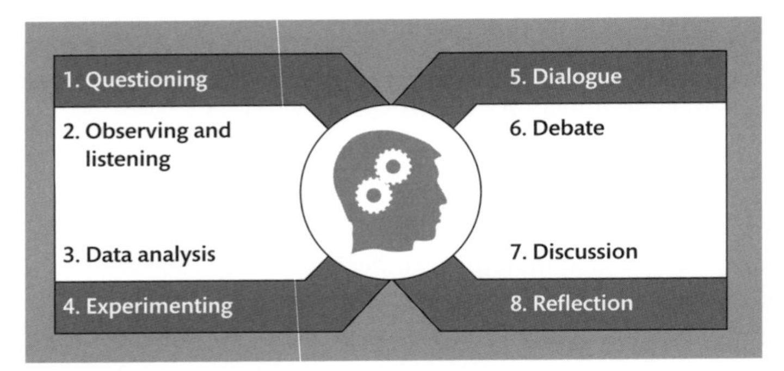

FIGURE 3.1 How to trigger strategic learning

(e.g. questioning) but which need to be reflected upon before learning really happens. Around the edges are the features of the type of environment that enables learning.

Within a learning environment, there are many things that can trigger valuable learning (see Figure 3.1).

Questioning

Peter Drucker, one of the most influential management thinkers, once said, 'the important and difficult job is never to find the right answers, it is to find the right question'. Questioning can be used to provide strategic insights and to test ideas. Skilfully used, questions can broaden our thinking and challenge the mental models and assumptions that are holding us back. A good question can provoke deep reflection and help us rethink our approach to an issue, and this process of questioning and reflecting is a virtuous circle that informs strategic thinking. One consultant's favourite question is 'What is the purpose of this organisation?' The initial, dismissive response of 'Well, it's obvious isn't it' usually masks a lack of clarity about why the organisation exists and its long-term direction. Most managers know *what* their organisation or team does, fewer understand *why*.

For all these reasons, skilful questioning is a rare but critical skill. In the context of strategy, it is helpful to think of three types of questioning.

Questioning assumptions

This means unearthing and challenging the mind-sets or mental models that underpin our decisions and opinions. Because our mind-sets cause us to filter out some things but pay attention to others, they can weaken our capacity to think strategically, resulting in strategic blind spots. And because mind-sets are usually unconscious, we may be unaware that we are neglecting potentially critical insights and information.

The Maginot line

The Maginot line was a powerful defensive fortification erected by France in the 1930s to prevent a potential German invasion. However, in 1940, the invading German army simply went around the Maginot line through neighbouring Belgium. The carefully constructed defences were redundant; directed against a type of attack that never came. The mind-set of the French generals, perhaps influenced by the previous war, caused them to overlook the real threat.

Similarly, in business, companies may fixate on competition from one source but overlook other, less obvious, threats.

We can use questions to tease out the unspoken assumptions that lie behind the views that people put forward. 'Why?' questions are very useful in this context, even if the questions may seem childish or too basic. Why are these your strategic priorities? Why are you investing in this way? What is your reason for wanting to grow? What did you take into account when you came up with that recommendation? What alternatives did you consider? If people become defensive or dismissive, persist, as you are almost certainly probing in the right area.

Questioning the methods

A manager's thinking can be constrained by what has worked in the past or by industry norms.

Britannia Food

In the 1990s, Britannia Food, one of the leading food and dairy producers in India, was pursuing growth. As a long-standing partner of Danone, its initial thinking was based around an approach that worked well in Europe, launching new higher-value products in cooperation with distributors such as supermarkets. But it became obvious that this approach would not work in India where distribution is much more fragmented. Instead, Britannia rethought its methods and came up with a range of products that offered a single portion or serving that people consumed in the street or within hours of purchase.

Even more importantly, they made use of the hundreds of thousands of street-based tradespeople in India, often operating from small tables on the streets, to sell the products. These tradespeople would buy the products from local distributors, renewing their stocks several times a day.

Britannia challenged the conventional method and found a way much better suited to its context.

Questioning the solution

It is tempting, once a seemingly feasible solution is found, to defend it resolutely. Truly strategic thinkers like to play devil's advocate and ask people to consider a diametrically opposite course of action. The aim is not to create conflict but to test the rigour of the thinking behind the proposed solution.

Observing and listening

Strategic thinkers spend time watching and listening. Like social scientists, they ask themselves 'Why do people do that?' The two-litre plastic soft drinks bottles we are now so familiar with were the result of someone noticing that many people struggled to carry large numbers of smaller bottles. This observation of something which had been going on for years provided an opportunity for innovation. Strategic thinkers pay attention to trends and things that are happening at the margins of society, because that is where fresh opportunities can be found. They deliberately seek out new places, new experiences and new people.

Travelling to discover

We know of two brothers, the President and CEO of a leading firm who put aside one month every year for travel. Despite already being world leaders in sports tracks and flooring, they spend time visiting partners, clients and suppliers, experiencing their culture, listening to their ideas and finding out how they see the world. For the two brothers, this yearly tour has been a source of inspiration for new products and an invaluable way of reflecting on the way they run the company. By listening to a wide range of people from different cultures and industries, rather than just the same old faces at headquarters, they open up their thinking to testing and challenge.

Data analysis

Data is neutral, with no intrinsic meaning. When it is interpreted, information can be extracted from the data which can be a source of knowledge and learning. But while data is neutral, the way we process and interpret it is full of filters and biases, mostly unconscious and undeclared. We tend to interpret information automatically, according to mind-sets and mental models acquired over time. It can be helpful to hit the pause button occasionally and think about how and why we are interpreting the data. Why do we focus on certain facts and figures? Why is data processed and presented in a certain way? A strategic thinker must be brave enough to challenge accepted 'truths' about data and how it is used. In order to ensure their thinking is robust, the strategic manager should seek out facts that challenge the accepted way of doing things and be willing to explore other possibilities.

Strategic thinking also demands that we consider the type of data used to shape decisions. Data can range from the purely quantitative (e.g. stock levels, numbers of staff) to the purely qualitative (e.g. impressions gained from talking with customers). It is a good idea to cross check between the various sources of data, testing conventional data, such as market surveys, against unconventional data, such as conversations with people outside the organisation.

Experimenting – learning by doing

There is no better way of triggering learning than by actually trying something out. Even if our expectations prove mistaken, rich learning is still available.

Thomas Edison, a prolific inventor, saw constant experimentation as vital. Commenting on yet another experiment that did not go as planned he said, 'I have not failed, I've just found 10,000 ways that won't work.'

Jeff Bezos has pursued a vision of a decentralised company where small teams can innovate and test out their ideas independently without going through a lengthy and frustrating process to gain permission. These 'two pizza' teams – according to Bezos, if you can't feed a team with two pizzas, it's too big – have created some of the Amazon site's quirkiest and most popular features such as Bottom of the Page Deals and the Gold Box – an animated icon of a treasure chest that opened to reveal time-limited special offers.

Dialogue, debate and discussion

In a world of fast-paced communication, instant messages and bullet-pointed 'get to the point' presentations, we are in danger of losing the art of dialogue. **Dialogue** is essential for enhancing our understanding of an issue, for highlighting biases and limitations in our thinking and for triggering creative thought. But it is a skill that requires awareness and practice.

Much communication in business is in the form of debate or discussion. A **debate** is a contest of ideas where each side looks for weaknesses in the other side's case and pushes its own proposition. A **discussion** is the examination of a subject, usually in order to solve a problem or agree a way forward. Both debate and discussion are essential parts of the strategy process. Debates can highlight the strengths and weaknesses of a proposal and discussion can be used to reach agreement on which solution should be adopted. But both of these modes of communication are limited in their scope. They do not lead to new understandings or new possibilities; they are convergent rather than divergent.

In contrast, dialogue is divergent by nature. It leads to an increase of ideas and understanding rather than the elimination of all but the dominant point of view. The word dialogue means, 'meaning flowing through', and instead of being competitive or defensive, participants in a dialogue are adding to each other's contributions so that their shared understanding deepens as the dialogue continues. Instead of trying to beat down other points of view, the participants use other perspectives to challenge and enhance their own thinking.

William Isaacs of MIT believes that 'dialogue seeks to have people learn how to think together – not just in the sense of analysing a shared problem, but in the sense of surfacing the fundamental assumptions and gaining insight into why they arise'. This surfacing of assumptions requires a context that encourages reflection and honesty, where contributions are listened to carefully and respected. As soon as the atmosphere becomes competitive or even combative, learning is in danger of being displaced by testosterone.

Strategic thinkers and their teams need to practise dialogue and intentionally add it to their communication repertoire. A prerequisite of dialogue is that all participants suspend their assumptions. This means not imposing their views or judgements on other people. It also means exposing or surfacing their basic assumptions for the rest of the group to examine. Different or opposing ideas must be welcomed and explored rather than forced to battle it out. In this way, each person's understanding of the issue is deepened, as is their awareness of their own biases and prejudices. As they open themselves to new perspectives, creative links can be made and new approaches generated.

Dialogue has many uses in business. It facilitates knowledge sharing and helps expose and challenge unhelpful mental models and blindspots. It can also build a deep sense of shared understanding, even when the participants start with different aims. But it requires time, skill and careful listening. Often it is helpful to use an external facilitator, particularly if the group is unused to this way of communicating. In the strategic process, dialogue is a wonderful way of fully exploring an issue and the way people are approaching it. Debate and discussion can then be used later in the process when proposals must be tested and choices made.

Reflection

The ability to critically reflect on one's thinking and experience enables a manager to continuously improve personal performance. However, the business environment is not always conducive to reflection. Hollywood and the popular press portray business leaders as energetic doers rather than reflective thinkers. TV series like *The Apprentice* emphasise decisive action over careful thought. The never-ending challenges and breakneck pace of organisational life put managers under great pressure and, as a result, they are often happy to do something, almost anything, rather than appear indecisive. But reflection requires time. And if the reflection is deep and challenging, the time will be repaid many times over. In shaping strategy, it is vital that the mental models we use and the way we 'frame' the problem are robust. Only through reflection, holding a mirror up to our own mental processes, can we assess if our thinking is fit for purpose.

Reflection is when we slow down our thinking in order to become aware of the mental models we are using and the way these models, or mind-sets, are influencing our actions. In reflection, we ruminate – or chew over – our thinking, examining it and looking at it from different angles. The result can be a new insight, a creative link, or a realisation that our thinking process requires some work.

Reflection is essential in the process of transforming experience into learning. It is obvious that experience, by itself, does not always lead to learning. If it did, organisations and people would be continuously becoming more knowledgeable, more effective and wiser. Sadly, this is not the case, and it is the absence or presence of reflection that helps determine whether or not experience is processed into learning.

Learning can be thought of as a continuous cycle of having an experience, reflecting on the experience, generalising or theorising about what was happening, and then applying or testing this new understanding in real life. All parts of the cycle are required, otherwise the learning process is short-circuited and we run the risk of never learning from experience. Without using reflection and the tentative theories that emerge from it, we would be like a science laboratory that constantly carries out experiments but never studies the results. There would be lots of activity but little progress.

Reflection is also the means to make sense of the complexity of the world we encounter. Problems do not come to us neatly labelled and separately wrapped. They are often intertwined and multi-layered, and sometimes do not at first seem to be problems at all. In such an interconnected and complex world, solutions that result from flawed or incomplete thinking, or even just habit and past procedure, can make things even worse. To be able to see the patterns and systems at work behind the events requires reflection.

Reflection can occur after or during the event. *Reflection-on-action* is when we go back over our experiences, turning them over in our minds and reliving them in order to find new learning. *Reflection-in-action* is when our learning is happening in real time. When we use an expression like 'thinking on your feet', we are referring to the ability to think about and refine our performance in the middle of doing it. Take the example of a group of jazz musicians improvising or 'jamming' together. They are listening to one another and adjusting what they play – as they play it. This ability to quickly respond to unplanned change is of obvious value in today's business world.

There are ways that reflection can be encouraged and practised. We have already referred to the value of questioning. Probing, open questions are excellent tools for reflection. Such questions could come from a mentor or colleague, or they could be part of a private, internal dialogue. Keeping a journal is also a good way of strengthening reflection-on-action. Interesting or surprising experiences can be noted down and then reflected on later.

The key messages of this chapter

- Learning is the process of transforming experience into purposeful action. The worth of experience resides on the change it provokes in our knowledge, skills or mind-set. Going from knowledge to mind-set the effort required and the impact increase. Mind-sets are spread rapidly within groups (and, therefore, within organisations) and, since they are deeply-rooted on our inner beliefs and values, they are extremely difficult to change. Changing a mind-set requires humility and openness to challenge.
- Some of the main triggers of learning are: questioning (concerning assumptions – mental models and mind-sets – methods and solutions), observing and listening, data analysis, experimenting, dialogue, debate and discussion as well as reflection.

ACTION POINTS

- It is worth reflecting on your ability to question assumptions, methods and solutions. When is the last time you challenged the status quo? If not in recent times, ask yourself why not and try to understand the key barriers that are revealed and how they could be overcome.
- Probing, open questions to mentors or colleagues are excellent tools for reflection. They could be part of a private, internal dialogue. Why not starting keeping a journal where you note down interesting or surprising experiences and reflect on them later?
- Finally, engage your mind into strategic thinking by taking long walks. Walking provides the perfect environment to reflect, develop ideas, connect the dots, etc.

4 What is business strategy?

DEVISING A STRATEGY is considered to be one of the most crucial activities in business, and it is normally seen as being something only done by the most senior people in the company. But in reality, strategy is something that is thought about and discussed in every part of the organisation.

You will no doubt have come across initiatives called corporate strategies, business unit strategies, marketing strategies, human resources strategies, information technology strategies and perhaps even more exotic creatures such as knowledge management strategies or corporate social responsibility strategies. Like many others you might be asking yourself if and how all these variants of strategy relate to one another. This was certainly the question we had when we first started working as strategy consultants.

Whilst they are clearly related in some way, it can be tricky to figure out the links and boundaries between the different types of strategy. For instance, where does business strategy end and corporate strategy begin? How does marketing strategy relate to information strategy?

In essence, strategy has different levels and different focuses (see Figure 4.1). The highest level is corporate strategy which addresses the questions of what business the whole company should be in and how the organisation should be managed

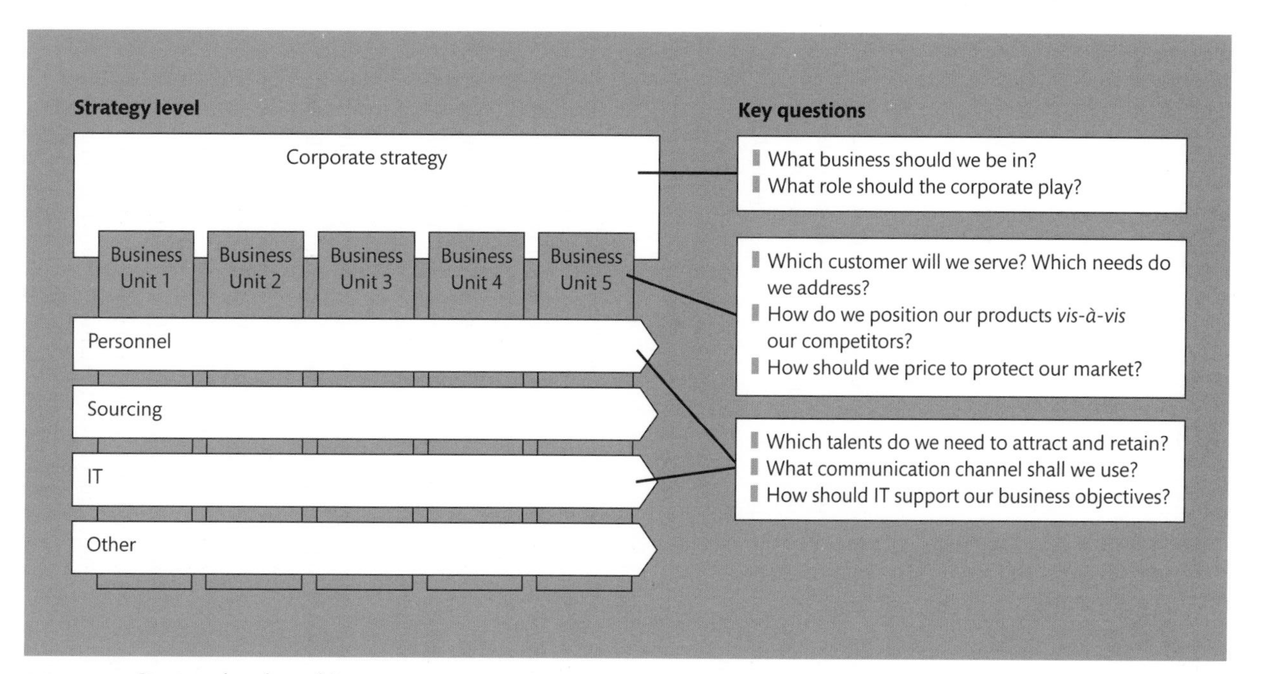

FIGURE 4.1 Strategy levels architecture

Source: based on McKinsey principles

and structured. Corporate strategy seeks to create value from the synergy between the elements of the business, so that the whole is more than the sum of the parts. Typical questions corporate strategy tries to answer are:

- In what business sectors should the organisation be involved?
- How much should the company invest in each of these sectors?
- What should the role of the corporate centre be?

One level down from corporate strategy is business or business unit strategy, which seeks to establish competitive advantage in each of the company's product or service markets leading to the creation of value in that particular business unit. This domain of strategy deals with questions such as:

- Which customers do we want to serve?
- Which needs do we want to address?
- Which products and services do we offer in response to the needs we have identified?
- How do we differentiate our products and services from those of our competitors?
- How should we price our products and services?

The last level is that of functional strategy. Marketing, human resources (HR), procurement, operations and information technology are all functions required for the achievement of business goals. Each of these strategies addresses questions specific to its area. For example, the HR strategy is driven by questions such as:

- Do we need more people? If so, how many do we need and what skills should they have?

- How can we increase productivity?
- Do we have succession planning in place?

The interplay between these strategies is important. In organisations operating in only one business sector, corporate strategy and business strategy are, to all intents and purposes, the same thing. For an organisation to be effective, there must be alignment between all levels and types of strategy. In practice this means that the objectives of each strategy should support, and certainly not obstruct, the aims of the other strategies. Misalignment is probably one of the main causes of strategic failure.

Imagine a firm where the strategy at corporate level is to pull out of a particular business sector. The person in charge of that business is developing a strategy to promote rapid growth through low prices. But, in the meantime, the marketing manager has crafted a sophisticated new branding strategy to raise the market positioning of the product. All three may be doing a great job in their separate areas, but lack of alignment will inevitably lead to disaster.

The importance of competitive advantage

As we explored in Chapter 2, strategy is defined as a set of coordinated, creative and sustainable actions (a plan) designed to overcome one or more core challenges that create value.

Value creation must be part of any strategy. Unless a company can generate enough value to cover the costs of delivering its products or services, it will not be in business for long. So value creation is a necessary part of strategy, but it is not, by itself, sufficient.

The strategy of a company should always aim to create *more* value than the industry average. After all, if a company provides only an average rate of return to its investors, they may well look for a better return elsewhere.

An organisation only has a **competitive advantage** when the outcome of its strategy, in terms of value creation, outperforms the average company in that industry.

Since the concept of value is multidimensional and always relative, we need to identify a convenient *measure* if we want to be able to compare an organisation to others in the same industry. **Profit**, and in particular the ratio of profit to the capital invested to achieve that profit, usually called **return on capital invested (ROIC)**, is a useful measure for value.

ROIC weights the profits a company generates versus all the funds invested in it, operating expenses and capital. Long-term ROIC tells you how well a company is using its resources.

In Figure 4.2 all the companies have made a positive return but only one, company V, has a ROIC that is clearly above average. Company V therefore has a competitive advantage. However, ROIC is just one measure of competitive advantage. Generally it works well but it can occasionally be misleading when comparing firms that have very different business models, such as one that relies on significant amounts of investment against one that makes extensive use of outsourcing and off-shoring.

In any industry, more than one organisation can enjoy a competitive advantage. There may be several – in Figure 4.2, companies II , IX and VI in addition to V the clear leader – with each probably pursuing a different strategy. In other words, there can be more than one winner and more than one way to win.

Simplistically, since competitive advantage implies that profitability is higher than the industry average this means that an organisation must command a higher price or operates

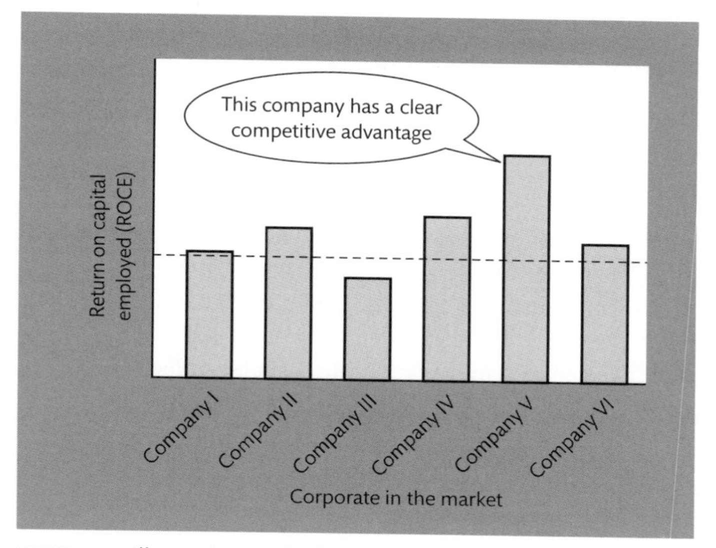

FIGURE 4.2 Illustrative profitability chart

Source: based on Porter, M. E. (1996) 'What is strategy?', *Harvard Business Review* (Nov-Dec): 61–78

at a lower cost, or both. Since competitive advantage is a relative measure (relative to the other firms competing in the same sector) we use the terms **relative price** and **relative cost**.

Relative price is the price of a company's product or service in relation to the market average. Similarly, relative cost is the cost of a product or service compared to the average cost of others in the same market.

Any given strategy will ultimately translate into a relative price and a relative cost. A positive difference between the two results in the creation of value, and a difference that is higher than average puts a company into a position of competitive advantage.

Competitive advantage is therefore a measurable result of what a company does, rather than its future potential or its greatest strengths. It is a result that is expressed in better than *average* profits. You may have great staff, a can-do culture and a cool brand, and these things are really helpful, but without the profits you do not have competitive advantage. But what if you are not in profit, or if your profits are below the industry average? If this is just a short-term blip there is no cause for alarm – yet. But you do need to start investigating what is going on. However, if having poor or absent profits is a recurring pattern there is no avoiding a diagnosis of no competitive advantage. This may not be what you want to hear, but it is best to know the truth so that swift action can be taken.

Because competitive advantage is about a result or an outcome, not just about potential, the first question companies need to ask is not 'What is our competitive advantage?' but 'Do we actually have a competitive advantage?' And if a company realises that it has no competitive advantage it can at least trigger a process to identify what needs to change.

How do you create competitive advantage?

So far we have talked about the importance of having a sustainable competitive advantage. The question now is how we build a competitive advantage in the first place. Competitive advantage is a great dish but we need the right ingredients (the sources of competitive advantage) and know-how to combine them – a recipe (the strategic options). Having either the best ingredients or a recipe is not enough, you need both.

The right ingredients: the sources of competitive advantage

There are many ingredients that can be used to build a competitive advantage. So we have grouped them into three categories: structural, execution and insight/foresight. Structural sources of competitive advantage are resources or assets that an organisation owns or controls and which cannot be accessed or copied by competitors. Execution refers to the superior efficiency and effectiveness of a company in utilising its resources. Insight/foresight is a superior ability to understand and anticipate the future. (A fourth source of competitive advantage is corporate culture, the deeply embedded belief systems and shared mental models that guide the decisions and actions of an organisation. But we will discuss this in more depth in Chapter 6.)

Structural sources

A structural advantage is something one company has that prevents other companies entering its market or competing effectively. It comes when, for structural reasons, competitors cannot copy a company's value proposition. It has been described as akin to a protective moat around the company.

Examples of structural sources

Structural sources might be any of the following:

- **Proprietary technology.** Google's rise to success was in large part due to a patented algorithm called PageRank that helps rank web pages that match a given search string.
- **An unrivalled access to a vital resource.** De Beers' long-held competitive advantage in the diamond trade, can be traced back to its ownership of the mineral rights to the vast majority of diamond mines.
- **Superior scale economies.** The Coca-Cola Company, through excellent plant capacity utilisation, achieves a cost of production that its competitors find almost impossible to match.

- **Low-cost manufacturing facilities.** ZTE, the up and coming telecom and mobile infrastructure provider, is becoming a formidable player in the market thanks to its access to high-quality, low-cost manufacturing.
- **A strong brand name.** Luxury conglomerate LVMH relies on the power of its brands such as Luis Vuitton, Puma and Bulgari to sustain its competitive advantage.
- **A large existing customer base.** Amazon is continuously conquering new market segments and offering new products and services to its ever-increasing and loyal customer base, which represents an asset difficult to replicate.

Execution

Some companies achieve their dominant position by consistently outperforming their competitors in the execution of their day-to-day business. High-quality execution allows a company to set itself apart from its competitors by performing better in critical aspects of its business system. This could take the form of delivering a superior or more convenient value proposition to its customers in terms of service or product features. Execution can be a source of competitive advantage when the following occur:

- **The entire business system is highly efficient.** McDonalds with its sophisticated franchising process, excellent staff training, careful selection of suppliers and remarkable global consistency in quality, cleanliness, taste and value for money has created a highly efficient and difficult to replicate business system.
- **Critical activities are executed distinctively**. Think of activities such as:
  - *customer service* for companies like Amazon that deal with hundreds of thousands of requests, complaints and other demands from customers that require an immediate answer;

- *workflow and process compliance* for companies like GE Capital where on a daily basis they review thousands of financing requests that require multiple checks to be carried out in a matter of minutes.
- *alignment of skills and incentives* for companies like Natura Cosmeticos of Brazil which manages a network of thousands of self-employed agents that sell its products.

Insight/foresight

Another source of competitive advantage lies in having unique knowledge or insight. This might be scientific or technical expertise, creativity or the ability to recognise patterns and trends.

Insight allows organisations to take decisions and implement activities based on a superior ability to understand and interpret data about the past. Take for example Amazon, who is able to recommend to individual customers, based on their past history with Amazon, products that they might want to buy. Features such as 'Frequently bought together' represent one of the most lucrative sales channels for Amazon. These features are built on insights into people's purchasing behaviour derived from the effective use of customer information.

Foresight, on the other hand, is the ability of organisations to anticipate future trends before they become mainstream. You might think that Madonna has access to a crystal ball, since for the past 30 years or so, she has been able to successfully anticipate and exploit many new trends in the music business. She has developed a remarkable ability in understanding the process of how innovations are gradually adopted by more and more people. In particular, she has learned how to spot new trends that have passed the first two stages of adoption (innovators and early adopters) and are about to reach the mainstream (see Figure 4.3).

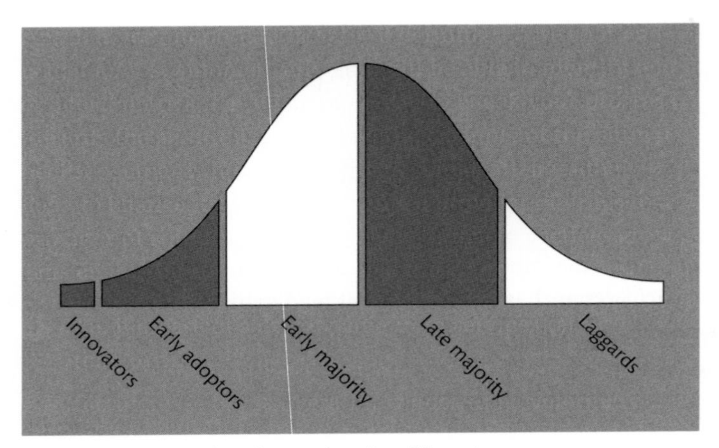

FIGURE 4.3 The technology adoption lifecycle

Source: Diffusion of Innovations, 5th ed., Free Press (Everitt M. Rogers 1962) Copyright © 1995, 2003 by Everitt M. Rogers. Copyright © 1962, 1971, 1983 by the Free Press. All rights reserved, adapted with the permission of Simon & Schuster Publishing Group.

Using insight and foresight enables organisations to anticipate trends and respond to them swiftly. These organisations are also better equipped to manage in conditions of uncertainty. They are tuned in to what their customers value and they can translate this knowledge into products and services.

A recipe: the value-creating options

We still need a recipe that will take some of these ingredients described above and turn them into competitive advantage. There are two fundamental recipes, or value-creating options: cost leadership and differentiation. Until recently it was believed that these two options were mutually exclusive. The advent of globalisation has changed such assumptions. Today we can find organisations that are able to pursue both options. We call this approach dual strategy.

Cost leadership

The **cost leadership strategy** is one designed to deliver products or services with features that are acceptable to customers and sold at a price that is in line with the average, but which the organisation is able to produce at a lower relative cost.

> **Cost leadership →** Relative price = Average and Relative cost < Average

A well-known example is the European airline company Ryanair. Ryanair has pursued a cost leadership strategy by eliminating all 'frills' and focusing on efficiency. For example, Ryanair makes its flight crew members buy their own uniforms and charges customers extra for hold luggage.

Even when facing large increases in fuel prices in 2006, Ryanair increased its profits. Its mission is to 'simply continue to be the Low Cost Leader in the European airline industry'. To achieve such impressive results, Ryanair has developed and maintained a business model dedicated to low-cost performance in every element of the value chain: quick gate turnarounds, non-union operations, performance-based incentive compensation plans, standardisation on one type of aircraft and flying (in most cases) to secondary airports.

Differentiation strategy

Does your product stand out from the crowd? Does something make the service you offer distinct from other similar products in the marketplace? Do your customers agree, and are they therefore willing to pay for this difference?

A **differentiation strategy** is a strategy that enables a firm to offer products and services that the end customer perceives to be unique, to the point that they are prepared to pay a relative price that is well above the average. Simultaneously, the firm is able to deliver such products and services with a relative cost that is in line with the industry average.

Differentiation ➔ Relative price > Average and Relative cost = Average

Excelling in the **specification** or **performance** of their product has allowed companies like BMW, Bosch and Geox to take up enviable positions in their respective markets where customers are prepared to pay extra. Geox makes much of its claim that its footwear 'breathes', due to technology based on intensive research and many patents. For the company, these are facts. For their customers though, it is all about perception and, happily for Geox, they agree and are willing to pay an above average price. Meanwhile Geox, thanks to economies of scale, global sourcing and operational excellence, is capable of delivering its value proposition at a cost that is in line with the industry average, and sometimes even lower.

Companies can also differentiate themselves by **brand**, by offering a product that provides an emotion through ownership. Brand has been described as the personality of a company or product and could involve the customer's perception of the trustworthiness, ethics, coolness, values or exclusivity of the company or its products. Examples of successful differentiation by brand include Ferrari, B&O and Tods. These companies, although they offer products and services with incredibly high standards and features, are able to deliver them with a cost structure that converts their premium pricing into high value for the company.

A culture of differentiation at Babolat

Babolat is a leading sports equipment company specialising in racquet sports. For the first 120 years of its history, the company focused only on strings, but in the 1990s moved to become a 'total tennis' company, producing racquets, bags, footwear and other tennis equipment. It now leads the market and 25% of the top players are equipped by Babolat. The success the company has experienced in recent years, expanding from just strings to a complete tennis equipment company, is the result of strategic thinking in pursuit of a clear intent: to become, and to be recognised as, the world leader in tennis equipment.

In the mid-1990s, the Babolat family business was doing well, but in a very niche market: strings and stringing machines. However, tennis as a sport was stagnating, with the number of players in tennis clubs in decline. Some well-known racquet manufacturers had already gone to the wall. Although others may have been tempted to diversify, Babolat decided on a different strategy, building on their core competencies and their understanding of the world of tennis.

In 1994 they launched their first racquets, followed later by tennis shoes (produced in partnership with Michelin) and other equipment. Many saw their strategy as risky. Eric Babolat, the company President, recalls 1994 as a 'crazy time' to start making racquets. But careful strategic thinking guided their successful expansion. For example, their racquets were produced in Taiwan in conjunction with a company with expertise in carbon fibre and composite materials. This enabled Babolat to differentiate itself from many of its competitors. Also, whilst most racquets were seen just as technical tools and came in colours like black or white, Babolat introduced more emotional associations by using vibrant colours and naming the different racquets according to the player's style (e.g. power, control). Another part of their strategy was to build relationships with younger players, signing Kim Clijsters at the age of 14, and Rafa Nadal when he was just 12.

Babolat's success was due to a clear strategic intent to build a differentiated positioning. It started with the Babolat family shaping the vision of becoming the uncontested leader in tennis sports equipment and then staying true to this vision through hard times. An attitude that combined relentless drive and ambition with humility and a readiness to learn from mistakes also played a major role in the company's success.

Babolat's differentiated proposition is clearly valued by customers who are ready to pay a premium to play with a Babolat racquet. In parallel, the company has successfully maintained a strong cost position leveraging long-term partners in Asia, both for production and technical innovation.

Dual strategies: achieving greater willingness to pay while keeping costs low

Achieving both a higher than average relative price and a lower than average relative cost has long been thought to be impossible. Michael Porter famously coined the term 'stuck in the middle' to describe firms that intended to follow both options but ending up failing to deliver competitive advantage. This is because a strategy of differentiation implies a high-quality offering, and significant investments in innovation, staff development and branding, which normally leads to higher than average costs. On the other hand, cost leadership calls for streamlined operations and high levels of standardisation and economies of scale. This normally results in a product which is not especially distinctive and which consequently cannot demand anything other than a relatively low price.

Recent examples, however, have demonstrated that a combination of cost leadership and differentiation strategies is not a 'mission impossible'. Take for example the case of Singapore Airlines who has been able to achieve a differentiation strategy but, intriguingly, without a cost penalty. In fact, Singapore Airlines is significantly more efficient than its peer group, a key feature of a successful cost-leadership strategy.

Singapore Airlines: a differentiated cost leader

The airline industry has been plagued by several factors such as overcapacity, commoditisation of offerings, cut-throat rivalry exacerbated by the entry of low-cost carriers, and intermittent periods of disastrous under-performance. Several factors such as rising oil prices, the SARS crisis, frequent concerns about the eruption of bird flu, the Asian tsunami and rising terrorism concerns have further adversely affected profitability. The industry is regularly rated as one of the worst-performing in the Fortune Global 500 rankings.

In this industry environment, Singapore Airlines (SIA) has consistently outperformed its competitors. It has never posted a loss on an annual basis, has achieved substantial and superior returns compared to its industry, and has received hundreds of industry awards for its service quality.

SIA achieved this outstanding market position by differentiation through service excellence and innovation, together with simultaneous cost leadership in its peer group.

Singapore Airlines' strategy

SIA is positioned as a premium carrier with high levels of innovation and excellent levels of service. The internal organisational practices, such as continuous people development and rigorous service design, are key aspects of operationalising and sustaining this positioning and strategic choice.

SIA has managed to deliver premium service to very demanding customers (achieving differentiation); at a level of costs that approaches those of a budget carrier. SIA supports this dual strategy of differentiation and internal cost leadership through the core competency of cost-effective service excellence, enshrined in a unique, self-reinforcing system of organisational processes and activities.

SIA's core competence is the ability to achieve a differentiated offering with exceptional levels of efficiency. This capability supports SIA's dual strategy, which in turn is aligned with macro environment and market conditions and is empowered by a strong consistent culture and adequate systems and processes.

Focus/niche strategy

A firm can decide to apply the three value-creating options described to all the segment of a market across geographic boundaries or decide to focus its effort and energy on a much more selected and limited scope. This could be because it does not have the resources to compete more widely or has identified a niche which, although small, offers a greater probability of success.

Firms like Ferrari adopt a differentiation strategy focus on the segment of super-exclusive high-performance sports cars which has only a very limited number of potential target clients worldwide. Bofinger Brasserie, a prime Parisian restaurant, adopts a differentiation strategy that is very focused on the Parisian seafood 'connoisseurs' willing to pay a premium for the highest-quality fresh fish. A local cement plant may adopt a cost leadership strategy because its economies of scale allows it to have the lowest cost of production within a 20 square kilometre area.

The key messages of this chapter

- Strategy has different levels and focuses. The highest level is corporate strategy which deals with questions relating to what sectors the organisation should do business in. Business unit strategy focuses on how to achieve a competitive advantage in each of the company's product or service markets. This will then indicate how functional strategies should be developed.
- At a business level, an organisation has a competitive advantage only when the outcome of its strategy, in terms of value creation, outperforms the industry average. Profit (and in particular ROIC) is a commonly accepted *proxy* to measure value creation.
- The sustainability of competitive advantage depends on the strategy's uniqueness and how difficult it is to copy.
- Organisations need to constantly look after their competitive advantage. Renewing it may be done in two ways: by continuous improvement and by transformation.
- Ingredients to achieve a competitive advantage may be grouped into three categories: structural, execution and insight/foresight. A fourth ingredient is the organisational culture.

- There are two fundamental recipes to achieve a competitive advantage: cost leadership and differentiation. A third option is the dual strategy which seeks to achieve both. If any of these approaches is applied to a distinct group in the market (instead of the mass market), then these are focus/niche strategies.

ACTION POINTS

- Think of organising with your team a workshop on competitive advantage, structured around the following strategic questions: do we really have a competitive advantage? What are its sources? Is it sustainable?
- Is your organisation trying to achieve cost leadership or differentiation, or both? This is another important question which calls for an answer. What facts actually support our cost strategy, are we really producing at a significant lower cost than the average in our industry? Or similarly, what facts support our differentiation strategy? Do customers really pay a premium to acquire our products or services? Do they recognise that we have a differentiated value proposition?
- Regarding the strategy development process, who is involved? Is it more collaborative or rather top-down? Try to reflect on how to increase the level of collaboration in the process. This could start by taking the strategic plan and organising a workshop in your department on how it could be cascaded down, or what it means to individuals with regard to their daily activities.

The strategic planning process

Fundamental to the development of effective strategy is the understanding that strategy is a process. The strategic planning process is not something that starts and finishes with the periodic production of a glossy strategy document. Unless there is a well-managed process that allows continuous learning, strategy is an exercise in wishful thinking. Over the years we have developed an approach to strategic planning called the strategic development process or **Strategy Roundabouts**. This is based on the strategic thinking process that we explored in Part 1, but this time it is a collaborative rather than individual activity.

We have tested the Strategy Roundabouts approach with all sorts of organisations, from multinationals to SMEs, and from not-for-profit organisations to family businesses. It has proven effective because it enables the members of an organisation to collaborate in the creation of effective strategy. The approach has six stages and in each of the next six chapters one of these stages is discussed in detail.

Just as strategic thinking should not be limited to the boardroom, effective strategy is a collaborative process, involving all levels of the organisation. Staff at the front line, working in sales or manufacturing, will have a practical understanding of customers and processes that a senior manager could never get close to. Therefore, the strategic process must be designed in a way that benefits from their insights and ideas. Also, the more employees are involved in

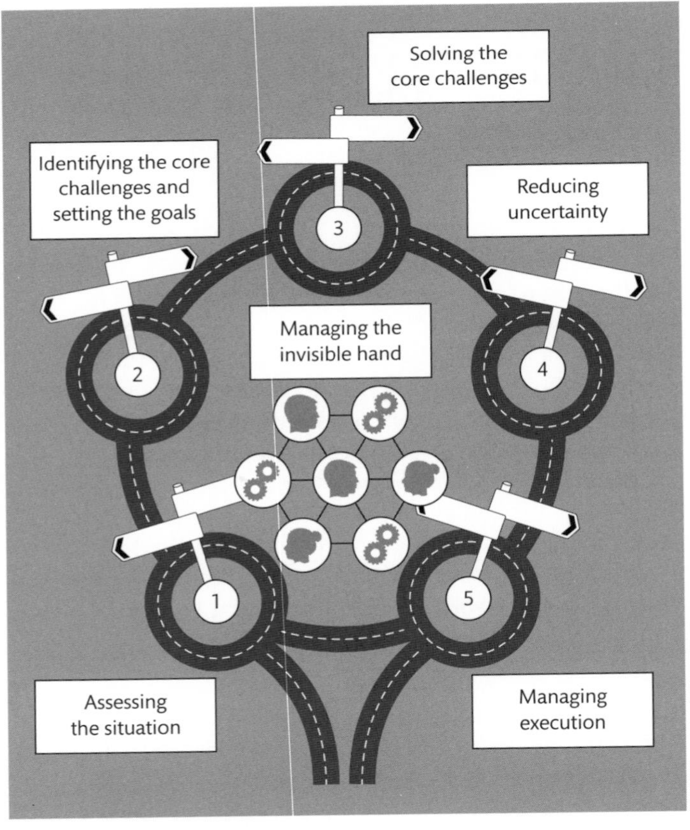

The strategy development process

Source: Sola, D., Couturier, J. and Scarso Borioli, G. 2013

developing a strategy, the more committed they are likely to be and the more they will understand the why as well as the how. If senior managers simply hand down strategy on tablets of stone and expect obedience, the best they can hope for is grudging compliance. A more likely result is failure, accompanied by a chorus of 'I told you so'.

It is the responsibility of the management board to define the vision, and there is a limit to the number of people who can be part of finally agreeing the future direction of the business. However the vision will be richer and more inclusive (and therefore more effective) if it comes from a genuine dialogue open to all staff. Genuine involvement takes time, but pays dividends.

5 Managing the invisible hand

THE FIRST STEP OF THE STRATEGY DEVELOPMENT PROCESS is what we call understanding and managing the invisible hand. It is perhaps misleading to call it a step since it is something that you will need to consider throughout the process. At every single stage it can and it will influence the process and outcome of the development and execution of strategy. It was Adam Smith, in the 18th century, who first used the phrase 'invisible hand' to describe the self-regulating behaviour of markets. But as you will discover, there is also a powerful invisible hand at work in the corporate setting, silently and effectively guiding and driving the decisions of each individual in the organisation.

Strategy development and execution is an activity that is particularly prone to the influences of the invisible hand. Many executives we encountered during our careers talked about their frustration due to strategy which seemed well conceived and well-crafted but failed not because of competitors or unforeseen events but because the invisible hand was not considered.

To help you to visualise the powers of the invisible hand we review recent events at Hewlett Packard (HP), the giant technology provider.

Hewlett-Packard (HP)

HP was founded in 1935 by Bill Hewlett and Dave Packard with a very clear purpose: 'to make technical contributions for the advancement and welfare of humanity'. HP experienced immense success that resulted in a constant double-digit growth.

HP's success was rooted in the firm's ability to constantly innovate and develop new products which produced profitable growth. This ability came from everyone's way of working. Every member of HP shared practices such as 'small bets' (promoting widespread experimentation and testing of ideas requiring little or no investment as opposed to big investment programmes) and 'management by walking around'. The firm had a way of thinking that emphasised 'fast learning by doing things rather than talking about them' or 'thinking ahead of the problem' and this remained part of the way HP worked even when Bill and Dave were no longer at the helm.

By the late 1990s incremental organic growth was no longer enough to deliver double-digit growth, or so HP started to believe. The result was that it started making bigger bets and growing by acquisition, such as its merger with Compaq in 2002.

A string of new CEOs including Carli Fiorina presided over a slow decline with strategies that never quite worked out. The culmination of this process was when Leo Apotheker was named CEO in 2010. His arrival from SAP with a track record of successes gave investors strong hope. He quickly crafted a strategy that would transform HP from a technology provider with a strong hardware core into an agile service firm anchored on a software core, targeting business and government markets. A number of key decisions were announced such as the possible spin off of the PC division, an exit from the smartphone and tablet business – and then the famous acquisition of Autonomy, the British search technology company.

This strategy was built on strong evidence and had the backing of investors, but it survived for only a few months. By the end of August 2011, Leo Apotheker was replaced by Meg Whitman (the former CEO of eBay).

So what made Apotheker and his predecessors fail in their quest to renew HP's ability to grow profitably? A large part of the answer can be found in the invisible hand's effect, which can also be referred as organisational culture (we will use the two terms synonymously). The strategic initiatives put in place by top managers did not fit HP's ways of doing things. Their fundamental error was not giving the right attention to the power of the company's invisible hand. The key learning from this story is that 'your vision will be resisted, plans will not get executed properly, and all kinds of things will start going wrong' if you forget to factor in the power of organisational culture.

What is the invisible hand?

Organisational culture (or the invisible hand) refers to the DNA of the organisation, the company's deeply embedded belief system and shared mental models, i.e. the way people have learned to interact with each other, with their partners and with customers. As we saw in Chapter 1, mental models are the source of our intuitions, enabling us to think and act very quickly and efficiently, though sometimes wrongly (i.e. when our mental models contain biases).

As individuals we develop 'scripts' over time as we repeatedly perform a certain task. The first time we carry out a task, we tend to think about every step and consciously consider the different ways the task could be performed. But over time, as we learn the best way to execute the task, we 'lock in' to a certain script, and the process becomes automatic. The result is that we keep going through the script every time we encounter that task or situation and we will not consciously think about each step again unless we experience a significant problem. But there is also a collective dimension to this that applies to teams and organisations. In fact, we can develop scripts without going through a step-by-step learning process, simply by copying or by being told how to perform a certain task by a member of the organisation. These communal scripts govern, like an invisible hand, the actions of groups in organisations, leading to unconscious assumptions about the way things should be done.

An organisation's belief system is the collection of mental models that are shared by its members. They have been invented, discovered or developed in response to problems. The fact that they produced an outcome judged to be good enough leads to them being stored in the corporate memory and transferred to all members as the accepted way of coping with similar problems. For example, if a manager has learned over time that increasing job satisfaction will increase employee performance, he or she is likely to do things that eliminate dissatisfaction among employees and works hard to increase their levels of satisfaction. When all managers of the organisation share the same mental models or theory, they are likely to make very similar decisions when solving problems. This leads to a consistent way of doing things and solving problems in an organisation.

Mental models include ways of diagnosing and solving problems, reacting to competitive moves, motivating people, dealing with customers and many other important aspects of decision making. The members of an organisation have a strong incentive to learn such mental models because it allows them to thrive (or at least to survive) during their time in the organisation. The stronger the collective mental models are, the less influence any one person's individual mental models will have.

Organisational culture is the sum of these mental models. We call it the invisible hand, since you cannot see the underlying mental models with the naked eye. If you ask someone about the different aspects of their culture they will probably struggle to give you an answer. The only way to uncover it is to 'observe the observable' and start with what can be seen: outcomes, visible artefacts and behaviours. Outcomes are the organisation's visible results such as revenue and the product portfolio. Visible artefacts include things like office architecture and dress code. Behaviours are the way people might deal with customers, develop new products or treat colleagues. However, these visible aspects will only tell you about the 'what' and the 'how' of organisational culture. They tell you nothing about why the organisation has chosen to do certain things and not others and why it has chosen particular ways of doing things.

Organisational culture is unique, and even organisations that appear very similar and operate in the same context will differ enormously in terms of culture. Also, there are often differences in culture between different departments within the organisation. This difference may be very large when, for example, the organisation is the result of a merger and two companies, each with its own embedded culture, are forced together. In fact, for many practitioners and scholars the difference between cultures is the major obstacle to successful mergers.

The role of culture in the success or failure of organisations is increasingly recognised as significant. Some have linked the demise of Enron with a culture that has been described as arrogant and lacking integrity, leading managers to decisions that resulted in catastrophic failure. Others have suggested that 'rogue' traders whose errors cost investment banks dearly are products of their culture, rather than exceptions to it. More positively, the successes of companies such as Wholefoods or Amazon, have been linked to cultures that emphasise trust and empowerment.

Strong and effective cultures

Famously, Jack Welsh argued that 'a company can boost productivity by restructuring, removing bureaucracy and downsizing but it cannot sustain high performance without a strong culture'. But what are the common traits of strong and effective cultures? As yet there does not appear to be conclusive evidence. However, we have conducted, over the years, a number of studies to try to highlight the aspects of organisational culture that most affect the ability of a firm to sustain its competitive advantage.

There are four things in particular that indicate the effectiveness of organisational culture: alignment, solidarity, execution and accountability, and renewal. Firms that have a sustainable competitive advantage tend to be strong in most of these areas, although no organisation can excel in all of them, simply because trade-offs will apply. For instance, if you are very strong in alignment this may be a deterrent to renewal, or if you are particularly strong in solidarity this may hinder accountability.

How to understand your corporate culture

The following are statements that can help you to describe your corporate culture. Try to apply them to your organisation and assign a score (0–5) to each statement where 0 would indicate strong disagreement and 5 strong agreement. Then repeat the exercise with colleagues from your department and some from another department. Finally, compare all the responses. What are the patterns and similarities within and between the departments? What are the differences?

Alignment

Alignment describes the extent to which people within the organisation share similar mental models and a sense of direction:

- I see my work as complementing the work of my colleagues.
- We are coordinated; we all wish to achieve the same goal.
- My role is part of an overall team plan.
- When I do not have particular direction or objectives I refer to the vision and the mission.
- There is value in sharing what I am doing and where I am going.

Solidarity

Solidarity explains how members of an organisation are prepared to help other members:

- I am loyal to my company and my colleagues.
- I believe in our mission statement.
- Better results stem from teamworking.
- If I see someone struggle I step in to help.

Execution and accountability

Execution and accountability describes the attitude of the members of an organisation towards making and executing decisions (as opposed to talking but never doing) and being accountable for the consequences, positive or negative:

- Once agreed it is done.
- We walk the talk.
- I think ahead of my task.
- If there is a problem I solve it; if I cannot I ask for support.
- Getting it done is more important than who does it.

Renewal

Renewal describes the ability of an organisation to challenge its assumptions and its beliefs, and its willingness to reconsider them all:

- New ideas should always be considered.
- I am not afraid to fail, difference is exciting, not dangerous.
- Without new ideas and different approaches we cannot survive.
- Innovation comes from listening to customers and employees.
- If I see that we are hitting a wall I should change direction.

Where does corporate culture come from?

It is very difficult to pinpoint one source that determines the culture of an organisation. Clearly the founding team contributes to the early formation of organisational culture. It achieves this in two ways. First, by hiring and retaining those employees who conform to its image of people with the right attitudes, behaviour and background. Second, it moulds these people, through role modelling, to its way of thinking and behaving.

During these early days the invisible hand is more evident, since it is totally embodied in the founders' view of the world, in their responses to everyday competitive challenges, and in their way of dealing with employees and customers. These ways of thinking and behaving can be organised along four dimensions – mission, vision, values and posture – although in the early days of the organisation these terms are unlikely to be used.

Mission

Mission is the reason why the organisation has been created. It provides a persuasive answer to the questions 'Why do we exist?' and 'What is our purpose?' The mission of an organisation is something that should resist the test of time and as such it represents the organisation's ultimate purpose. An organisation cannot exist without a mission, and all organisations have one. (There are many mission statements on the web, for example www.missionstatements.com has Fortune 500 companies' statements, amongst others.)

Sometimes the mission is implicit and completely embodied in the founder's way of doing things. At other times, particularly in firms that have undergone a period of soul searching, it is much more explicit. If a company intends to change strategy (i.e. to enter new sectors or launch a particular activity) it needs to make sure this is in line with its mission.

Vision

Vision is the envisioned future. It is a loose description of how the world would be better if certain challenges are overcome. A vision helps anyone dealing with the firm to visualise its ultimate destination, the ultimate goal. This is the destination that may be achieved one day, perhaps quite far in the future. Take for example Sony's vision that was set in the 1950s (see below). It clearly describes the challenges that Sony intends to overcome (i.e. create products that become pervasive, become the first Japanese company entering the US, succeed with the transistor radio, etc.) as well as the ultimate goal: 'Made in Japan will mean something fine, not something shoddy.'

Vision is an excellent way of describing and sharing the direction of an organisation, but having one is not essential. Organisations can live without a statement of vision and indeed there are many who have thrived without it. For example McKinsey, the renowned strategy firm, has never developed a vision. Its invisible hand works around its mission and values.

An example of vision: Sony

We will create products that become pervasive around the world. ... We will be the first Japanese company to go into the US market and distribute directly. ... We will succeed with innovations that US companies have failed at – such as the transistor radio. ... 'Made in Japan' will mean something fine, not something shoddy.

Values

The values are the principles that guide the behaviour of people in the organisation. They represent what in a free society are the rules of just conduct that help to determine what a good citizen should be. Values (see below) are the basis of trust. A person can only trust another if they share, at least to some degree, the same set of values. If the level of trust is low then the normal reaction is to increase control. This explains why highly dysfunctional organisations, where people do not share any values and therefore do not trust each other, are often very bureaucratic, full of procedures and checks. Sharing values and therefore having a high degree of trust ultimately helps people to work collaboratively without fear that they will be taken advantage of, or be burdened with bureaucratic procedures.

An example of values: Microsoft

As a company, and as individuals, we value:

- Integrity and honesty
- Passion for customers, for our partners, and for technology
- Openness and respectfulness
- Taking on big challenges and seeing them through
- Constructive self-criticism, self-improvement, and personal excellence
- Accountability to customers, shareholders, partners, and employees for commitments, results, and quality.

Having said many positive things about mission, vision and values, a note of warning should be sounded. Unfortunately, such statements are often no more than statements. This is because they either do not reflect the real mission, vision and values, or worse, they are just wishful thinking.

Posture

A final determinant of the corporate culture that derives from the founders is posture. Posture is the general attitude that an organisation has towards certain types of strategic decisions. Posture, at least at the beginning, is the reflection of the founders' view of the world. However, it can change over time as the external world or the organisation's configuration, including its leadership, changes. There are usually four types of posture: shaping, adapting to the fastest, reserving the right to play, and exiting.

- Organisations adopting a **shaping posture** want to exercise leadership in the way the industry operates, driving it towards a new structure that they influence. This could be done by shaking up a relatively stable market or by trying to determine the way a more uncertain market develops. Netflix have been rewriting the rules of the video-on-demand market by offering unlimited access to a huge range of movies at a low, fixed price. This has disrupted the industry and wrong-footed other players such as the telecom operators who have invested in a pay-per-view model.
- **Adapters** take the current industry structure as a given and react to the opportunities the market offers. In markets with a high degree of predictability adapters carefully choose where and how to position themselves in order to compete within current industry constraints. In more uncertain markets, their strategies are based on their ability to spot and respond quickly to developments. Reebok displayed this ability in the way it successfully adapted to Nike's reshaping of the sneaker/sports apparel market into a lifestyle-driven industry.

- **Reserving the right to play** is a non-committal posture. It is sometimes a response to situations currently in a state of uncertainty but which may offer opportunities at some point in the future. It involves making incremental investments aimed at putting the company in a privileged position in future. By doing this, the company seeks to keep its place at the table, until the situation clarifies enough to allow a more positive strategy. This was the approach of many companies in the early days of the internet. They initially made modest investments to give themselves a presence on the web and then added to this as the significance of the internet gradually became apparent.
- **Exiting** is a decision to withdraw from the market and redeploy resources elsewhere. Exiting is to some extent an admission that initial hopes have not been realised. It can be a blow to company pride and those with something to lose from the exit are likely to be critical. Practically, it is recognition that the environment turned out to be different to what was expected and that there are other opportunities where the company's resources and capabilities could be more profitably employed. There may also be a cost of exiting, in the form of redundancies or assets that cannot be redeployed.

  Suzuki's exit from the US car market after 27 years was an admission that the Japanese company had never won over American consumers in the way that Honda and Toyota had succeeded in doing. But exits do not always indicate a struggle for profitability. Pfizer decided to leave the animal health business, despite enjoying comfortable margins, because it wanted to focus investment on its core pharmaceuticals business.

The final contributor to the formation of organisational culture is internal and external shock. Internal shocks could be a sudden change of leadership or any event that leaves its mark on the firm. Think for example about a firm changing the CEO or the majority of the management team and replacing them with outsiders. Or consider the repercussions of a sudden change in regulations or the advent of a new technology that revolutionises the way the firm must work and compete (external shocks). Both types, although sudden, will have a lasting impact on the way employees work. It may take time and the effects may not be visible at first, but the culture will be affected and the invisible hand will guide in a slightly different way.

How does it become visible?

As we have discussed in the previous section, the power of the invisible hand can be observed through the artefacts and behaviours visible in the organisation. These are the vectors that transfer corporate culture to new members and across time (see Figure 5.1).

Leadership and role modelling

One of the most obvious ways for organisational culture to become visible and to transfer across people and time is through **leadership and role modelling**. For example, if leaders advocate that innovation is the crucial factor for the company to sustain its competitiveness, then a symbolic act such as an open door policy to encourage people to come forward with ideas will tell employees much more than any grand proclamation made but not followed up in reality.

Governance and organisational structure

Another very visible manifestation of the invisible hand is the **governance and organisational structure** of a firm. Simply put, governance and organisational structure describe the roles, responsibilities and decision-making powers, relationships and interactions, and channels of communication between the different stakeholders

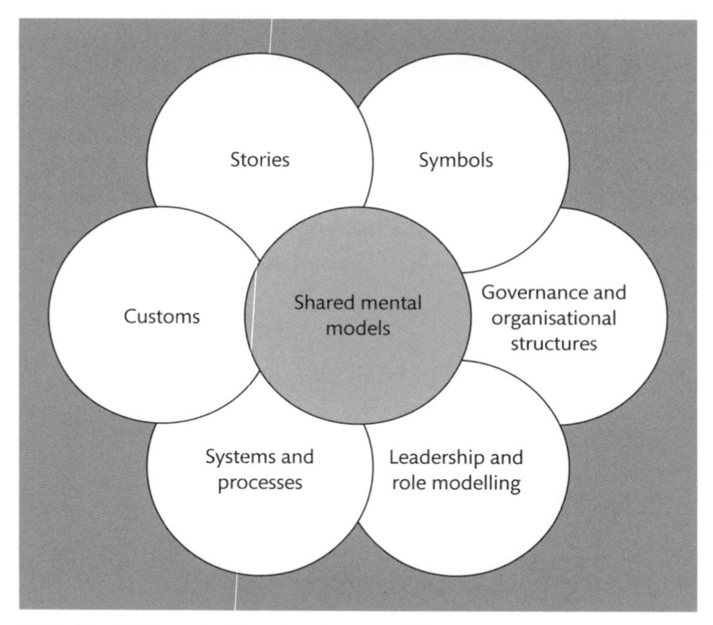

FIGURE 5.1 Organisational culture architecture

Source: based on Johnson, G. (1987) *Strategic Change and the Management Process*, Blackwell

(employees, executives, board members, customers, suppliers, investors, etc.). Governance and organisational structure are highly visible signalling devices for organisational culture, providing helpful clues as to the nature of the invisible hand. For instance, a very open, flat and accessible governance model will clearly signal that collaboration is key, that decision-making is devolved, that diversity is accepted and that leadership is won through trust and performance rather than based on someone's position in the hierarchy.

Customs, stories and symbols

Another manifestation of corporate culture which is particularly effective in transferring culture to new entrants is **customs** and **stories**. A custom can be defined as 'a long-established practice or ritual considered as unwritten law'. Customs dictate the manner of conduct a company's employees are expected to follow. They prescribe the etiquette to be observed in dress, speech, courtesy and politics. These norms are established to project a particular image the company wishes to convey.

Stories have the powerful feature of revealing meaning without committing the error of defining it and they connect rationally and emotionally. Storytelling is a traditional means of passing on wisdom and culture. Stories pass from the top to the bottom of the organisation, from one function to another. They are transmitted through generations of employees and carry with them a powerful implicit lesson. Stories and storytelling help to convey norms and values within the organisation and also to the outside world. A great example of this is the Zappos culture book (see below).

Stories are potentially very effective in developing trust and commitment. For example, stories that get told around the organisation about the behaviour of managers will shape people's views about whether managers can be trusted much more powerfully than any official values statement. Stories are also good at sharing tacit knowledge; the all-important but unwritten 'know-how' possessed by effective employees. Because the knowledge is embedded within an engaging and memorable story, tacit knowledge about problem solving or dealing with particular situations can be transmitted far more effectively then by formal teaching techniques.

Systems and processes

Last but not least, culture becomes visible and it is transferred across people and time via **systems and processes**. In general terms, systems are the tools that enable the organisation to produce products and services. In an organisational setting, systems are variously used to set goals, to measure performance, to evaluate leadership, to reward and recognise people and to share information. Processes are just collections of related, structured activities that produce a specific service or product for a particular internal or external customer.

The nature and purpose of the systems and processes in an organisation will provide important insights into its culture. If you are a software company and believe that providing leading-edge technology is one of your core values, you will put in place those systems to measure this dimension. Eventually you will also design a reward system that encourages technological innovation. In an organisation where employees are trusted and empowered, you will not see lengthy and formal approval processes but you will notice advanced information-sharing systems to allow people to take decisions at all level. Also, routines or procedures can become so embedded that they themselves become part of the culture. Systems and processes that are particularly important in preserving and transferring culture are recruitment and training.

Zappos: where culture is the most visible source of competitive advantage

This is the firm that revolutionised the shoe retailing market. Zappos has consciously decided what its corporate culture needs to look like and it deliberately reinforces and supports this culture on a daily basis. Its 10 core values are embodied in all aspects from employee job descriptions to the hiring process, from on-the-job training to the day-to-day work environment. Those values span from 'deliver WOW through service' and 'create fun and a little weirdness', to 'be adventurous, creative and open-minded'.

Zappos takes cultural fit seriously and hires slowly. Months can pass between an initial 'cultural fit interview' and an actual job offer. If you are hired by Zappos, you can expect to spend your first three or four weeks manning phones in the call centre, learning how to respond to customer needs. While this is an introduction to the soul of the business, it is also a practical approach to serving customers all year long. Upon completion of their time in the call centre, Zappos employees are offered $3,000 to leave the company. If you haven't become a Zappos insider, committed to the goals and the culture, the company really prefers that you leave. But if you take the money, you can never come back.

Each manager is expected to spend 10–20% of the department's time on employee team-building activities. These activities include an Easter egg hunt put on by the shipping department. Performance evaluations at Zappos reinforce the culture. Managers do cultural assessments rather than performance evaluations and give employees feedback on their fit within the culture and how to improve. In an environment that gives pay rises based on skill tests, this makes sense.

Zappos has a culture book that is written by employees every year. It details how people feel about the Zappos culture and how they reinforce and develop the culture every day. Statements attributed to employees emphasise and reinforce this culture.

This case shows how one company has responded to the challenge of preserving and transferring its culture. For many organisations such a conscious approach to culture is not a priority, particularly in fast-growing organisations. This is very worrying since in growing companies, ensuring the cultural fit, for example of new employees, should be a major concern. It is during their first days within the new organisation that new employees are the most receptive to cultural signals.

How can you manage it?

The culture of an organisation can act as a sort of magic wand which makes it successful, innovative and highly-regarded. But it can also be a horrific invisible enemy that threatens the very survival of the company, as in the case of Hewlett Packard.

Going back to the HP story, you might think at this stage that there was nothing Apotheker could do. That, although Apotheker knew the way forward, it was impossible to beat the culture and that HP was unlucky because, instead of the magic wand, it got the invisible enemy. But this thinking is incorrect and fatalistic. Determining whether culture will be a magic wand or an invisible enemy is not something just in the lap of the gods. Although it will take time, the invisible hand can be managed and shaped. This is possible because the invisible hand consists of deeply embedded patterns in how people work together that have proved successful in the past and which employees instinctively follow.

Managing culture means a change of culture, which can occur either as a result of a crisis – 'the burning platform' – or through evolution. In the first case the organisation is facing a situation of change or perish that forces people into rapid cultural adaptation. The second case is where one or more forward-thinking executives realise that the sorts of problems to be confronted in future will be very different from the ones it now faces. For this reason they begin the process of adaptation.

Both cases require the entire company to reflect on its underlying shared assumptions and mental models. Open discussions talking to colleagues, suppliers and customers about their impressions of the company will help. Compare what you find with the assumptions that characterise a strong culture listed earlier in this chapter. And while leaders cannot control culture, they can certainly influence it. What leaders say, and especially what they do will have an impact. The things they pay attention to, the way they respond when mistakes are made or risks are taken, the behaviours that they reward or punish, all have an impact on the culture.

In situations requiring a cultural evolution to cope with new challenges such as the need to drastically reduce time to market or moving from providing product to providing services, one approach is to create a separate team. This team is asked to address the new challenges and figure out effective ways of dealing with them. Once it has developed new and successful ways of working, the team is not disbanded. Instead other staff are asked to join, a few at a time. As they pick up the new ways, culture change begins to spread.

It is important to remember that it is very risky, if not counterproductive, to make cultural change your core challenge; the one problem that you need absolutely to resolve if you want the firm to succeed. Tackling culture is best done indirectly: use a business core challenge to reshape the culture and not the other way around.

An example of reshaping the culture

A new CEO comes into post and finds a culture that is not well suited to the challenges now faced by the company. Perhaps the company evolved as a quasi-monopoly and developed a culture of passively serving customer demand. But now, because of deregulation, it needs to fight for every customer. Here the CEO and the management have two options. One is to declare that radical change in the way the company works is necessary and to present a logical case for change. Alternatively they could identify a process such as re-examining how the company interacts with customers. As they involve the staff in redesigning the systems and activities that will be more successful in actively winning business they have, in effect, begun the evolution of a new culture.

The key messages of this chapter

- Though we identify 'understanding of the invisible hand' as a first stage of the strategy development process, this is something that has to be considered throughout the process.
- The invisible hand refers to the culture of the organisation. For organisational culture, we mean the deeply embedded belief systems and shared mental models.
- There are four important attributes of effective organisational cultures: alignment, solidarity, execution and accountability, and renewal.
- Mission, vision, values and posture are embodied in the invisible hand.
- Organisational culture becomes visible and is transferred across employees in many ways: leadership and role models, governance and organisational culture, customs and stories, systems and processes.
- The invisible hand can be managed and shaped, though it takes time. A change of culture can occur as a result of a crisis – the 'burning platform' – or through evolution.

ACTION POINTS

- Organise a get-together and ask each participant to perform the 'How to understand your corporate culture' exercise. Then ask people to discuss the results with a colleague; then ask all participants to share their views. You may discover some very interesting insights!
- Are you clear on your vision, mission and values? Are they mostly theoretical ones that are part of the 'official' package, only seen once with your welcome pack and then forgotten? Or are they really easy to spell out and in everybody's mind?

- Do you have a clear vision of where the company should be in the next 5–10 years? No one who claims to be a manager can elude this question. It is time to put some ideas on the table and share or test them with those around you.
- Do you think you act and behave in sync with the desired culture of your organisation? Are you seen as a role model? What about others? Perhaps it is time to have an offsite retreat on the themes of alignment, solidarity, execution and accountability, and renewal, focusing on how to make the organisation's values the normal way of doing things.

6 Assessing the current situation

STRATEGY IS ABOUT DEVISING ACTIONS that will help create value and maintain or increase competitive advantage in the future. But before thinking about future actions we need to understand how what we are already doing, and the decisions we have already taken, are affecting value creation and competitive advantage. A strategy that does not take into account the starting point is a strategy without foundations.

A willingness to review its actions and decisions is a sign of organisational health. It triggers questions, dialogue and reflections that could generate ideas about improving or even completely re-thinking the organisation's business systems. This chapter explains the first stage of the strategy development process, aiming to help you to assess where you are and how your current strategy creates, or inhibits, competitive advantage. This calls for an in-depth understanding of many different elements, both within and outside the organisation, and their interplay.

These elements and the relationships between have been synthesised into a framework: the **competitive advantage ecosystem** or **CAES** (see Figure 6.1).

The two outermost squares cover the company's external environment consisting of the macro environment and the competitive environment or industry structure. Analysing

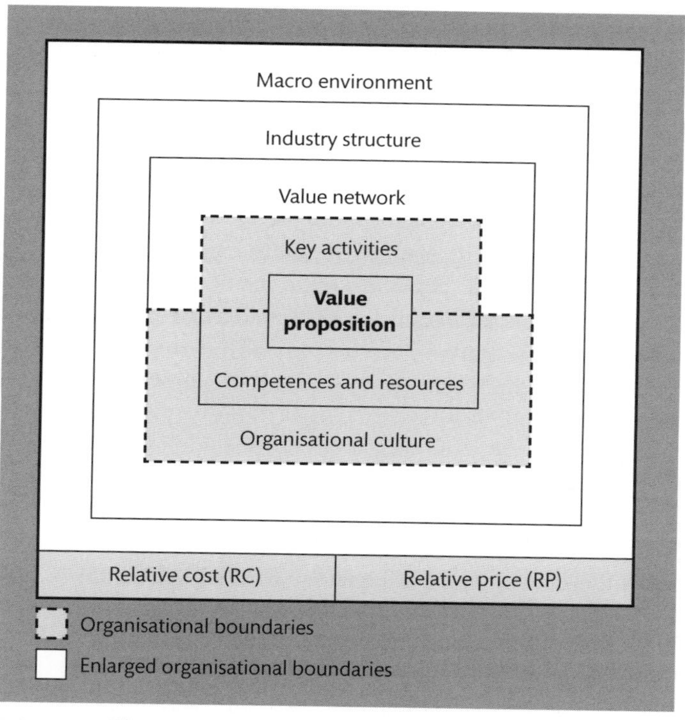

FIGURE 6.1 The competitive advantage ecosystem (CAES) framework

the macro environment helps to answer questions such as 'Are we in the right place?'; investigating how the industry sector one has chosen to compete in compares to other sectors. Analysing how the industry you are in is structured will help you understand the performance variance of different businesses within your sector as well as how value is distributed between the different stakeholders. Overall, the aim of analysing the external environment is to establish if you are in the right place and see how your current strategy is performing compared to those of your competitors.

The areas within the organisational boundary (the dotted line) are those covered by your business model analysis, also referred as the internal analysis. The business model analysis focuses on understanding what drives your current strategy and how you have configured your business systems to respond to the demands of the competitive environment. It looks at the decisions you have taken about activities and resources and how these decisions were taken, including the role played by the invisible hand or organisational culture. Business model analysis is centred around the **value proposition**, which is the sum of the benefits that the organisation promises to deliver to its customers, through its offering, for which those customers are willing to pay. This includes the products and services that you have decided to provide.

Delivering a value proposition requires a number of activities to be performed. The ones that the company has decided to manage directly we call **key activities**. These usually include primary activities such as procurement, design and engineering and production, as well as support activities which help improve the effectiveness or efficiency of primary activities such as research and development, legal services and human resource management. These key activities require two inputs: **resources and capabilities**. Resources are the key production factors, both tangible (e.g. capital, infrastructure, human capital) and intangible (e.g. patents, brand, corporate culture). Capabilities are the skills and know-how that the company has developed over the years in performing the key activities.

A value proposition also requires activities, resources and capabilities that the organisation decides to ask someone else to supply or carry out on its behalf. The collection of external businesses or individuals that contribute to the delivery of the company's value proposition is called the **value network**. Members of this network can range from businesses that may also supply other companies, including your competitors, to exclusive or joint venture partners.

The value proposition, and the activities, resources, competences and value network that create it, are linked and glued together by the **invisible hand** (see Chapter 5). The way the company organises its activities internally, the tacit know-how that exists in its employees, and the set of shared values, will influence the relationships the company builds with its value network and how it manages the components. The organisation culture is the 'oil' that lubricates the mechanisms of the system and enables the organisation to deliver value to its customers.

The CAES framework sets out all the components you need to configure and how they relate to the organisation's value network in the context of the competitive environment and the overall macro environment. The task of executives is to design or redesign these components in order to achieve one of the two value-creating options: **differentiation** (i.e. increasing customers' willingness to pay while keeping costs around the average), or **cost leadership** (i.e. achieving lower than average costs while being able to achieve prices around the average).

Finally, the CAES framework helps by forcing those involved in the strategic process to make explicit their assumptions about where the business currently is. As these assumptions are shared and discussed, they will lead to the challenging questions and reflections that will guide the company towards continuous improvement or even transformation.

Are you in the right place?

A good way to start is to review the performance of the different industries that form an economy and see how your industry's performance compares to these. This analysis will trigger questions and reflections about why certain sectors are performing better than others and what factors contribute to this difference (see Figure 6.2).

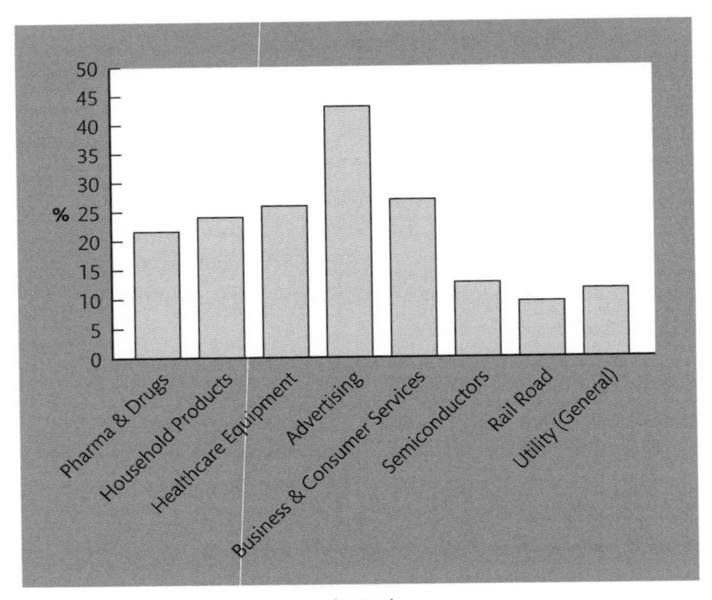

FIGURE 6.2 ROIC per industry (2012)

Source: 3H Partners (2013), Damodaran Online (excluding US companies)

For instance, if you are a business located in the pharmaceutical industry certain factors must be affecting your sector in a beneficial way to produce a return on invested capital (ROIC) that is nearly three times that of the transportation sector (rail road).

You can then go on to compare the performance of the different sectors over a number of years. Profitability can fluctuate in the short term for a number of reasons so an historical view provides a more reliable long-term picture of the relative performance of the various sectors (see Figure 6.3).

In Figure 6.3 we can see that in 2012 some industries experienced a contraction while, in others, performance did not change significantly from that in 2011.

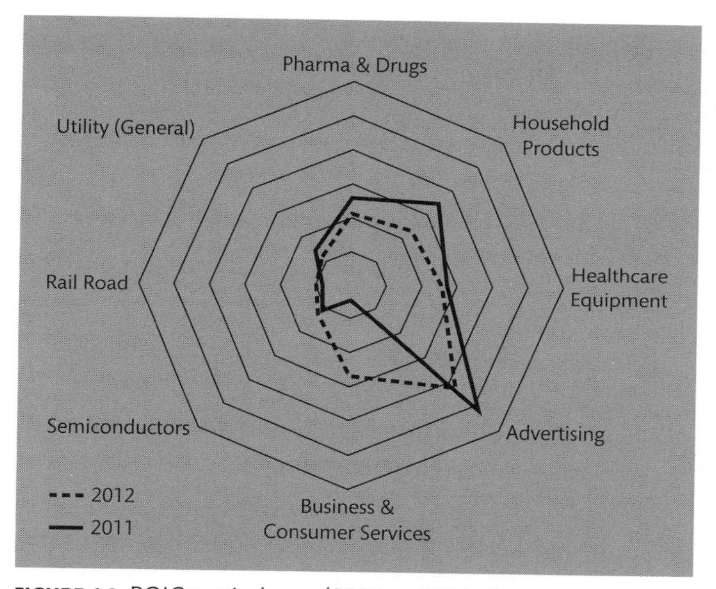

FIGURE 6.3 ROIC per industry (2012 vs. 2011, illustrative)

Source: 3H Partners (2013), Damodaran Online (excluding US companies)

What could account for this sort of difference in performance between sectors over time? There are two types of factors that could explain such differences: macro-environmental factors and industry-related factors.

Macro-environmental factors

The macro-environmental factors that influence the performance of a business sector can be explored using the widely known and used PESTEL (political, economic, social, technological, environmental and legal) framework:

- **Political:** factors relating to government policies or decisions (planned or being taken) that could influence positively or negatively one or more business sectors. For example, if a government decides to open up trade in a particular sector, this will impact upon businesses operating in that sector as the number of new entrants rises and competition increases.

- **Economic factors:** these refer to the overall outlook of the economy, the GDP growth rate, unemployment, inflation, etc.
- **Social:** factors in the social macro-environment like demographics and changes in culture. For instance, increasing average life span in many countries has had an enormous impact on industries such as pharmaceutical and healthcare, and changing patterns of immigration will influence workforce supply and consumer behaviour.
- **Technological:** these are factors such as new technologies that give rise to innovative products and services and disrupt the status quo. An obvious example of this is the way that the development of the internet has affected how music and video are accessed by customers. Music and video retailers such as HMV and Blockbuster have learned to their cost how quickly and how profoundly technological change can reshape an industry.
- **Environmental:** factors that directly or indirectly affect the physical environment such as the exploitation of natural resources like water, oil and gas, and the ever-growing problem of waste management. These factors are having an impact on most sectors but on some the effects are very visible. The tsunami in Japan caused a national disaster but also affected the energy sector around the world as governments grew more nervous about nuclear energy and put their investments on hold.
- **Legal:** this refers to laws and regulations, and the loopholes that companies can find, that could affect how an industry works and performs financially. A recent and controversial example is how companies like Amazon and Starbucks have exploited loopholes in taxation laws to increase their profitability by reducing the amount of tax they pay.

Ultimately the macro-environmental factors will always affect the cost and price of goods and services, and therefore increase or decrease the profitability of a sector. Table 6.1 illustrates this for the airline industry. Of course, any single factor can have multiple effects, positive and negative, on both price and cost. Deregulation in the airline industry, which has opened it up to a number of new players, has had a negative impact on prices as intense competition has driven them down, and it has also had a negative impact on costs by creating a structural over-capacity where there are more planes and flights than required, thereby increasing airline costs.

As illustrated in Table 6.1, the various factors have had conflicting effects on the industry. On one hand, deregulation has allowed newcomers to enter the industry. Budget airlines

TABLE 6. 1 The PESTEL framework for the airline industry

Factors	Factor description	Impact on prices	Impact on costs
POLITICAL	Deregulation	↓	↓
	Stop 'state aid'	↑	↑
ECONOMIC	Increase in oil price	↑	↑
SOCIAL	Terrorist attacks	↓	↑
	Increased travelling	↓	↓
TECHNOLOGICAL	Web ticket sales	No direct impact	↓
	Bigger aircrafts	No direct impact	↓
ENVIRONMENTAL	CO_2 emissions restrictions	↑	↑
LEGAL	Labour law requirements	No direct impact	↑
	Immigration checks	No direct impact	↑

like Ryanair and easyJet barged into the sector and increased the overall 'offer'. Higher competition and increased choice resulted in downward pressure on prices. Other factors, such as the increase in oil prices, the public fear of terroristic attacks and the withdrawal of state subsidies have had serious negative consequences for players in the airline industry. Companies that have been smarter, in terms of anticipating and taking prompt action in response to these factors, have suffered less and have been more effective in taking advantage of other, more positive, emerging factors such as web technology and the way it can streamline customer interactions.

Industry-related factors

Macro-environmental factors can explain some of the variance in performance between different sectors, but for a fuller picture we need to look at the forces at work within an industry:

- **Intensity of rivalry** in an industry determines the intensity of the competition between the players. If rivalry is very intense, organisations are likely to pass more of the value they have created to customers in the form of lower prices or increases in quality without raising prices. Alternatively, they may invest more in R&D in a search for new products that will give them an advantage in the market, or poach staff from their competitors who will hopefully bring valuable expertise or know-how.
- **Bargaining power of customers,** who are always happy to pay less and get more. Powerful buyers will force prices down or demand more value in the product, thus capturing more of the value for themselves. When customers increase their buying power, even in conditions of moderate rivalry, value will transfer their way.
- **Bargaining power of suppliers** who are seeking to be paid more and to make their clients more reliant on the goods or services they provide. Powerful suppliers will charge

higher prices or insist on more favourable terms, thereby lowering industry profitability. Microsoft and Intel for many years enjoyed an enviable level of bargaining power over computer manufacturers who were completely undermined in any negotiation by the power of the ubiquitous Windows software and Intel microchip architecture.

- **Threat of new entrants** to the sector. Companies often try to erect barriers to prevent newcomers taking a slice of the market. The mobile technology industry has enjoyed healthy returns for many years, and this has triggered the interest of potential new players who are trying to enter the market. Increasingly one can see that the incumbents are fighting back by protecting their intellectual property (i.e. patents), one of the strongest barriers to entry a company can build.
- **Threat of substitutes** – products that could replace, under certain conditions, the core product of a business sector. Substitutes can put a cap on industry profitability. A good example of the power of substitutes is the market for travelling between Paris and London. Eurostar enjoys a great advantage over alternatives such as travelling by air or by bus. An average Eurostar return ticket is around €300 for a two and a quarter hour journey as opposed to a flight that costs around €180 but takes four hours (with check-in, etc.) or a bus ticket costing €50 for a seven-hour journey. These prices are the result of the competitive interplay from the different alternatives. But if train fares increase much beyond their current level, a number of customers will consider switching to a substitute service such as air or bus travel.

The study of these forces and their interplay was the seminal work of Michael Porter, to the extent that the framework that represents them is usually known as **Porter's five forces model** (see Figure 6.4). The model explains the industry average prices and costs and therefore the average industry profitability, providing a baseline for measuring competitive advantage.

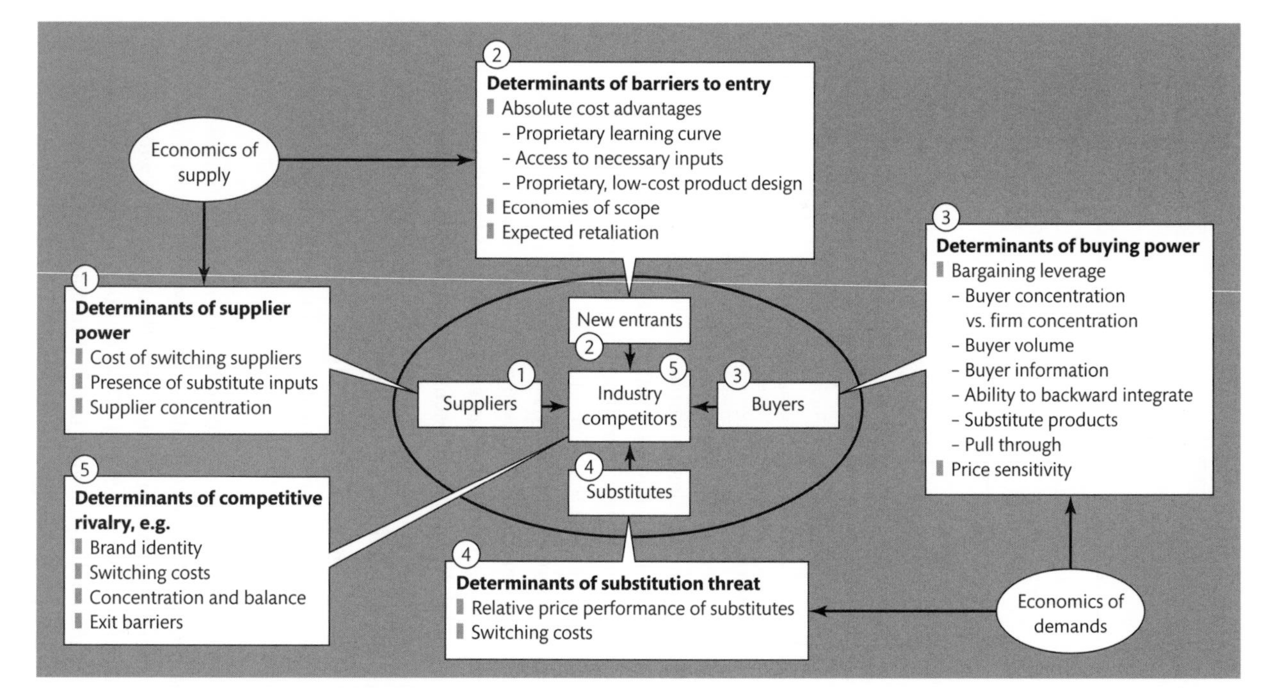

FIGURE 6.4 Porter's five forces model

Source: adapted from Porter, M. (1980) *Competitive Strategy: Techniques for Analysing Industries and Competitors*, The Free Press adapted with the permission of Simon & Schuster Publishing Group.

TABLE 6.2 Impact of Porter's five forces on industry profitability

Force	**Level**	**Impact on industry profitability**	**Average price**	**Average cost**
Intensity of rivalry	High	↓	↓	↑
Bargaining power of suppliers	High	↓	No direct impact	↑
Bargaining power of customers	High	↓	↓	↑
Threat of new entrants	High	↓	↓	↑
Threat of substitutes	High	↓	↓	↑

Source: adapted from Joan Magretta (2011) *Understanding Michael Porter*, Harvard Business Review Press, p. 41,

Each of the five forces has an impact on industry profitability. Table 6.2 shows how the level (high or low) of each force influences profitability. Take the force of intensity of rivalry. You can see that if intensity of rivalry is high then the profitability of the industry will be dented. This is due to average prices being driven down coupled with a potential increase of costs as spending on advertising, R&D, etc. goes up. The model does not give each force a specific weighting in terms of how it affects profitability. All the forces need to be assessed individually, and for each force the main influencing factors need to be identified and evaluated. Only then would you be able to allocate a weight to each factor and therefore give a weight to each force.

There are two important points to be made here. First, the average profitability of a business sector will be determined by the interplay between Porter's five forces and the wider macro-environmental factors (PESTEL) that we looked at earlier. The benefits of a very favourable macro environment could be completely wiped out by a very unattractive situation within an industry sector, and vice versa. Also, these analyses are snapshots of one part of the whole system at a single moment. It is important to put them in a larger chronological and systems context.

While carrying out each analysis you need to ask yourself questions that locate it within the wider context: Is the current situation sustainable? How might current competitors and new entrants influence the way the industry is structured? Could something happen which would disrupt the industry? Are there opportunities to expand beyond the current boundaries of the industry?

Only by thinking in this way will you be able to move from having a snapshot of how things were at a point in time, to seeing a moving picture of how a sector or even an economy is developing over time. This enables you to identify emerging trends and future opportunities.

Do you have a competitive advantage?

Using PESTEL and Porter's model we can begin to understand what the overall average profitability of an industry sector is – the baseline. The next step is to investigate how all the players in that industry are performing. Any average is composed of elements that are greater and elements that are lesser. Likewise an average profitability is made up of players whose profitability is below the industry average and others whose profitability is above it.

An example from the pharmaceutical industry

If we look at a subset of companies operating in the pharmaceutical industry we find that not all companies obtained the same results during 2010 and 2011. Figure 6.5 shows that Celgene enjoyed the highest ROIC during this period, although the level sharply decreased from 2010 to 2011.

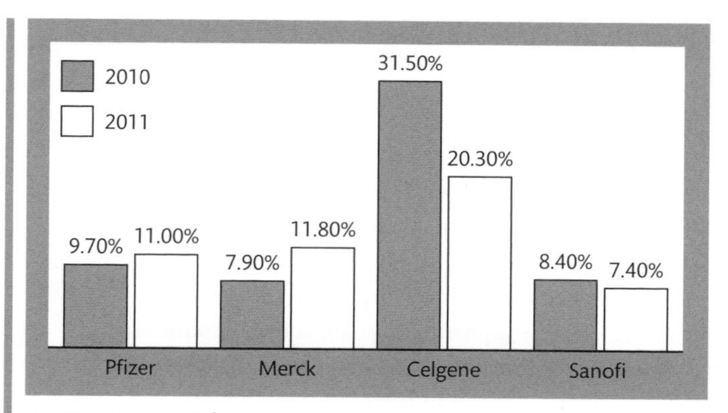

FIGURE 6.5 ROIC for pharmaceutical companies

Source: 3H Partners (2011), Damodaran Online

To understand why there is such difference within an industry we need to compare the performances. In particular, we need to investigate which of the available value-creating options (i.e. cost leadership, differentiation or dual strategy) the different players have adopted and whether they are aiming at a mass or niche market.

There are three progressive levels of analysis we can do to quickly evaluate differences in profitability between players (including your company) in an industry: net operating profit and invested capital; average cost; and average price.

Take the hypothetical case of three firms belonging to the same industry who all perform differently as regards ROIC. Applying the three levels of analysis we first need to identify the **net operating profit (NOP)** and the **net invested capital** of each company.

In Figure 6.6, company A has a 10% ROIC, which can be calculated as NOP ($11m)/Net invested capital ($110m). Also while company A has an higher ROIC than company B, the latter has better operating profits, which means that company B is using its capital less efficiently than company A. Company C appears to be the most efficient in this group.

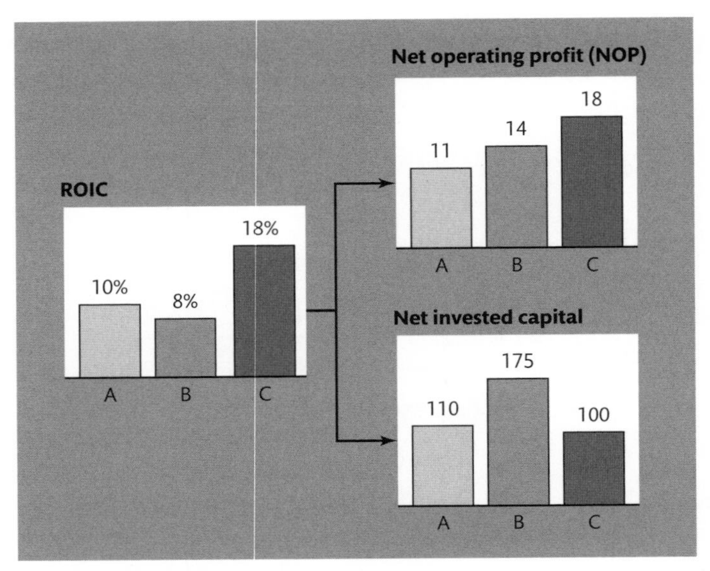

FIGURE 6.6 Breakdown analysis of ROIC

Now we need to see how company C achieved its superior NOP. By breaking down the NOP into its constituents – revenue and cost (see Figure 6.7) – and performing an **average cost analysis** we can see that company C has lower revenues and costs when compared to the others.

Using the last two levels of analysis, **average price** and **average cost analysis**, which involves investigating further the revenue side and the cost side by breaking it down into volume and average price (see Figure 6.8) and average cost (see Figure 6.9), we see that company A has the biggest slice of market share (in terms of volume), followed by company B. Company C, although having the lowest volume, has been able to impose very high prices (60% more than B) but keeping cost proportionally much lower (only 49% higher than B), indicating that it may be pursuing a differentiation strategy as a value-creating option.

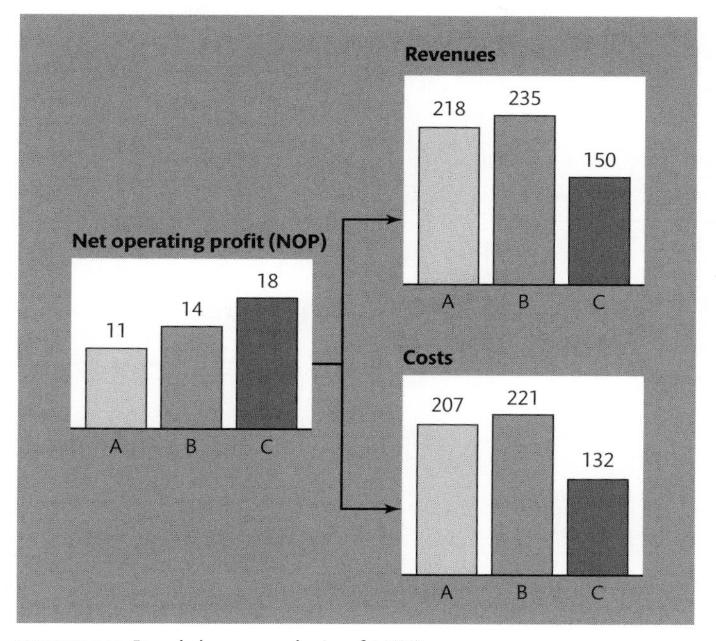

FIGURE 6.7 Breakdown analysis of NOP

Putting all the evidence from our three levels of analysis together, we can see that company C has a competitive advantage thanks to differentiation.

These are high-level analyses that will provoke further questions and suggest further, more detailed analytical work. It is always worth investigating how company performance has varied or developed over the years. Profitability is the result of many factors and can change suddenly. For this reason it is important to ask whether the performance of a company has been consistent and whether its current performance is sustainable. It is also important to know whether there is too much reliance on a product nearing the end of its life cycle or whether the company has launched a succession of new products.

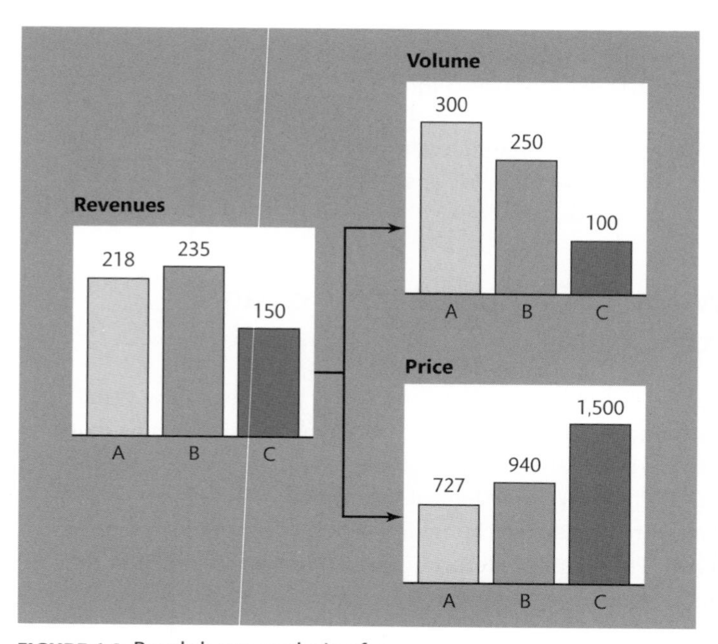

FIGURE 6.8 Breakdown analysis of revenues

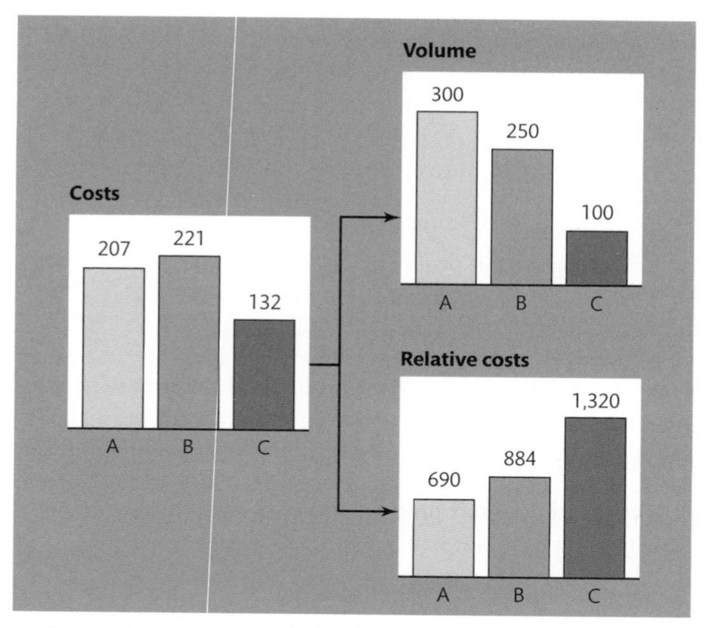

FIGURE 6.9 Breakdown analysis of costs

The simplicity and wide applicability of these analyses make them helpful in generating clues and insights about how firms within the same industry perform so differently. They will not tell you why this is so, but at least they will point you towards the answers.

Where does superior value creation come from?

By this stage you should have a better picture of how your performance compares with other companies and some clues about which value-creating strategic option each company has adopted. We now look at our business model and its configuration, so we can review whether changes need to be made. To do this we return to the CAES framework, and the inner sections in particular (see Figure 6.1 earlier).

Value proposition

The cornerstone of any business model is the value proposition, which is the sum of the benefits that the organisation promises to deliver to its customers through its offering, whether products, services or both, for which customers are willing to pay.

Defining the value proposition of a company starts with listing the categories of products and services that it is currently offering. Then, for each product or service, the following five groups of questions must be answered:

1. What is the product's scope and uses? What are its key features?
2. Who is this product aimed at? Where are the customers?
3. What need does our product address? What problem is it trying to solve? Is it a significant problem for the

customer? To what extent does the product address the problem?

4. How is the product delivered to the customer? How do customers find out about the product? Which distribution channels do you utilise?

5. What is the product's price position? What is the cost position (i.e. relative price versus relative cost)?

The **first group of questions** helps in defining the boundaries of the company's market and clarifying in which markets the company is currently competing. A business could have products that, without modifications, could be sold in very different markets.

Motor oil example

A classic example concerns motor oil. Is the motor oil used in cars part of the same industry as motor oil used in heavy trucks and stationary engines, or are these different industries? The oil used in cars is similar or identical to the oil used in trucks. However, motor oil for cars is sold to a fragmented, generally unsophisticated group of customers, through numerous channels, using extensive advertising. Products are packaged in small containers and logistical costs are high, necessitating local production. On the other hand, truck and power generation lubricants are sold to entirely different buyers in entirely different ways using a different supply chain, and the industry structure is substantially different.

Automotive oil is thus a different market sector from oil for trucks and stationary machinery. Profitability differs between the two sectors and a lubricant company will need a separate value proposition and strategy for competing in each area.

The **second group of questions** concerns customer and market segmentation. A market segment is usually defined as a group of customers who have similar needs that are different from customer needs in other parts of the market. Traditionally, relevant criteria for segmentation include:

- demographic/socioeconomic (e.g. gender, age, income, occupation, education, household size and stage in the family life cycle);
- psychographic (e.g. similar attitudes, values and lifestyles);
- behavioural segmentation (e.g. occasion of use, degree of loyalty);
- product-related segmentation.

It also deals with the dimension of geography. Most industries are present in many parts of the world. However, for your industry, you need to consider whether competition takes place within the boundaries of a particular state or region or whether, like some industries, competition takes place on a global stage. If the industry structure for two products is the same or very similar (that is, if they have the same buyers, suppliers, barriers to entry, and so forth), then the products are best treated as being part of the same industry. If the industry structures differ significantly the two products may be best understood as being in separate industries.

The purpose of the **third group of questions** is to clarify the problem that the product or services is trying to solve, or the need it is designed to meet. It is estimated that out of 30,000 products launched every year based on very strict ideas about product scope and market segmentation, 95% fail. Simply aiming a product at a certain market segment does not guarantee that customers will buy it. A customer uses or 'hires' products and services to get a job done that needs doing. So identifying your target customers starts with understanding what jobs they need to get done, which will differ from the job served by other segments.

A milkshake's jobs

Clayton Christensen, a Harvard Business School professor, tells the story of a fast-food restaurant chain that wanted to improve its milkshake sales. The company started by using marketing experts to come up with the profile of a typical milkshake-drinking customer. Next, it asked people who matched this profile to list the characteristics of their ideal milkshake (thick, thin, chunky, smooth, fruity, chocolaty, etc.). The would-be customers answered as honestly as they could, and the company used the feedback to modify their milkshakes. But milkshake sales did not improve.

Christensen's fellow researchers approached the situation by trying to find out what 'job' customers were 'hiring' a milkshake to do. He discovered that 40% of the milkshakes were purchased first thing in the morning by commuters who ordered them 'to go'. 'Most of them, it turned out, bought [the milkshake] to do a similar job,' Christensen writes. 'They faced a long, boring commute and needed something to keep that extra hand busy and to make the commute more interesting. They weren't yet hungry, but knew that they'd be hungry by 10 a.m.; they wanted to consume something now that would stave off hunger until noon. And they faced constraints: they were in a hurry, they were wearing work clothes, and they had (at most) one free hand.'

The milkshake was 'hired' in lieu of a bagel or doughnut because it was relatively tidy and satisfying, and because trying to suck a thick liquid through a thin straw gave customers something to do with their boring commute. Understanding the job to be done, the company could then respond by creating a morning milkshake that was even thicker (to last through a long commute) and more interesting (with chunks of fruit) than its predecessor.

Source: 'Marketing Malpractice: The Cause and the Cure', *Harvard Business Review*, Vol. 83, No. 12, December 2005.

At this point you might ask why companies continue to use mainly 'classical' market segmentation criteria such as demographics. The answer is that they already have the data which allows them to do this. Again, the right starting point is finding out the job that your customers want to get done. Once you have identified the job-to-be-done, you have to be creative in working out how you can address this need in a *unique* way. Deciding how you will help customers get the job done is a crucial step and goes far beyond deciding the features and details of your product or service. You also need to decide how your product will be delivered to your target customers (e.g. online, through physical stores, through department stores, etc.).

It is important to note that an organisation should offer different value propositions in the different *industries* in which it operates. This means that the organisation needs to be clear about the boundaries of the different 'fields' it is playing in. Understanding boundaries is a tricky issue.

Apple and its crossovers

In the digital era, it has become normal for the boundaries of many industries to change and evolve over time, creating crossovers within industries that were apparently unrelated. Those boundaries evolve at a pace that was unthinkable 20 years ago. The most emblematic example was provided by Steve Jobs during the early 2000s. During the 1990s, Apple Computers Inc. was an American company operating in the computer industry, and its geographic scope encompassed the different territories in which it was offering its products. In 1999 something happened which, on the surface, was irrelevant to Apple: Napster started offering an illegal file-sharing service which quickly became very popular before it was shut down in 2001. Napster had demonstrated that consumers were more than happy to swap their CDs and DVDs for downloads and that there was an unmet need for this. The Napster experience, combined with Jobs' entrepreneurial genius, was enough to either revolutionise or destroy the boundaries across seven industries: personal computers, movies, music, phones, tablet computing, digital publishing and music/video retailing.

> Jobs ignored the conventional perception of the boundaries between these industries, seeing the eventual digitisation of all industries that produced and transmitted content: publishing, film, music, radio and TV. The web was the catalyst and enabler that would speed up this process. In 2002, digital storage surpassed non-digital storage for the first time and by 2007, 94% of storage capacity in the world was digital. On 9 January 2007, Jobs announced that the company would now be known as Apple Inc., because computers were no longer its main focus.
>
> Jobs had created a company, later to become the most valuable in the world, that did not fit into any specific industry pigeonhole but had created crossovers between and among different industries which are still evolving. Instead of obsessing about how to make a better PC, Jobs saw that his customers wanted a new 'job to be done' and asked how he could exploit Apple's skills and resources to help them. Customers were looking for a greater amount of easily accessed entertainment and, by ignoring industry boundaries, Jobs provided them with a solution.

Apple is perhaps the most high-profile example. However, it would be wrong to think that crossovers only apply in the area of digital information. The current wave is all about 'things' – your car, house, electrical grid, etc. And companies like FedEx, P&G and GE are seeing traditional boundaries in their industries changing at a very fast pace.

The **fourth question** relates to how the value proposition is delivered, and there are many ways of doing this. The Four Seasons hotel chain is an example of how companies can choose to directly manage most or all of the activities and processes right up to the point of utilisation by the customer. This Canadian company offers its high-quality services through managing all its own operations, including buildings and staff, with little or no outsourcing. Other companies, such as Micro Scooter of Switzerland, make extensive use of external suppliers and partners to deliver their products while they focus on particular areas of expertise, which in the case of Micro Scooter is design and engineering. It relies on others for activities such as sales, product assembly and marketing.

The **final question** concerns pricing and costing. The price a company attaches to its value proposition is the one component that most easily triggers intuitive decisions on the part of customers. How many times have you looked at a product offering and made a rapid judgement of its quality based on its price? The price positioning of the value proposition can act as the starting point of the value proposition development process. For instance, if you have observed that a group of customers were over-served and therefore overcharged, you may decide to develop a value proposition that can win these customers by eliminating unnecessary features and charging less. This is called *unbundling*. A good example of this is the way low-cost airlines strip back their offering to its bare essentials.

Conversely, some companies target customers who are underserved and who might be prepared to pay extra for a more comprehensive service. The quality of life services firm Sodexo recently launched its Welltrack service aimed at employees working in remote locations such as oil platforms. As well as high-end catering services, Welltrack also offers fitness activities, counselling and life coaching to help staff cope with the stress of being far from home and family. Although much more expensive than a traditional catering service, Welltrack's benefits go beyond providing nutrition. In the sites using Welltrack, absenteeism has been significantly reduced creating an enormous impact that goes beyond the additional cost of catering.

Key activities

Creating a product or a service involves carrying out a number of activities. As part of the development of your value proposition, you need to scrutinise all the activities that are required to bring it to your customers in order to understand how each activity contributes to value creation and at what cost. Ultimately, you must ensure that the value created exceeds the costs incurred in creating the offer.

Take a critical look at which activities are crucial in creating your value proposition. This is important because, in most circumstances, you will not wish to relinquish control of these activities – your **key activities**. Other activities, however, are less significant in terms of their contribution. These are the ones you might decide to allocate to suppliers or partners, perhaps because they can perform them more cheaply or more effectively.

The **value chain model** developed by Porter can be very useful in understanding how value is created or lost in terms of the activities undertaken by the organisation.

As you can see from Figure 6.10, Porter divides the activities needed to create the product or service into two main categories: primary activities and support activities. **Primary activities** are *directly* concerned with the creation or delivery of a product or a service and can be grouped into five categories:

- *inbound logistics* – the activities concerned with receiving, storing and distributing the inputs, including materials handling, stock management, transport, etc.;
- *operations* – includes all activities that transform the various inputs into the final product or service (e.g. machining, packaging, assembly, testing, etc.);
- *outbound logistics* – concerned with collecting, storing and distributing the product or service to customers, including warehousing, materials handling, distribution, etc.;
- *marketing and sales* – provide the means whereby customers are made aware of the product or service and are able to purchase it (e.g. sales administration, advertising, etc.);
- *service* – includes those activities that enhance or maintain the value of a product or service (e.g. installation, repair, training, etc.).

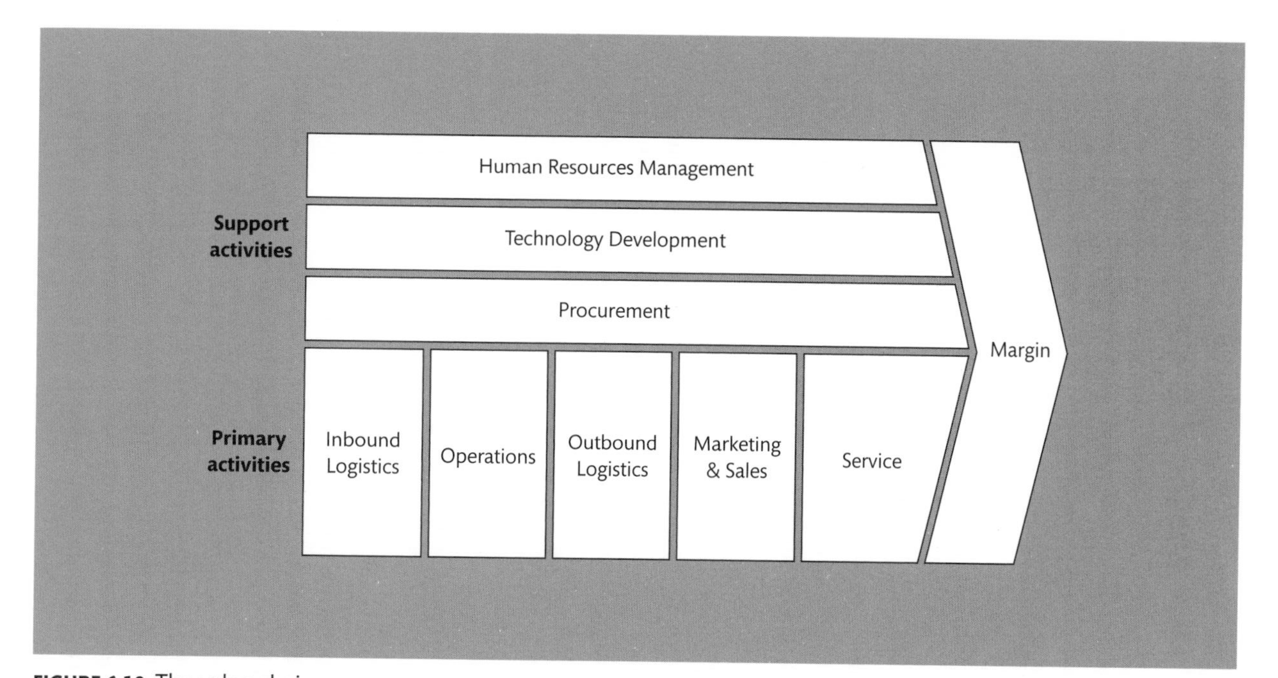

FIGURE 6.10 The value chain

Source: adapted from Porter, M. (1985) *Competitive Advantage: Creating and sustaining superior performance*, The Free Press, Copyright © 1985, 1998 by Michael E. Porter. All rights reserved, adapted with the permission of Simon & Schuster Publishing Group

Support activities are those that improve the effectiveness or the efficiency of primary activities:

- *Procurement* – the processes for acquiring the various resource inputs to the primary activities – occurs in many parts of the organisation.
- *Technology development* –'technology' is used here in its widest sense to encompass 'know-how' as well as more formal design activities. Technology development could apply to researching and designing products, developing efficient processes or working with raw materials.
- *Human resources (HR) management* – this is a particularly important area that transcends all primary activities. It is concerned with all subjects linked to HR from recruiting, training, managing, developing to rewarding people within the organisation.
- *Infrastructure* – this encompasses all systems, structures and routines that affect the organisation's performance (e. g. the systems that support planning, finance, quality control and information management). It also includes organisational structure.

Mapping the organisation's activities is not a descriptive exercise. It should be used to think hard about the ability of the organisation to perform each activity. The analysis should trigger questions such as:

- Which value-creating activities are especially significant in meeting customers' needs (i.e. in terms of 'getting the job done')? How can I usefully develop them further?
- To what extent and how does the organisation organise and manage its activities in a *unique* way?
- What aspects of value creation are difficult for competitors to replicate because they are embedded in the company's systems, structures and culture?

- Which activities, today considered to be crucial, may not be crucial tomorrow? If this happens, how will I rearrange my value chain accordingly? For instance, production of CDs was believed to be a crucial activity for value creation for companies such as EMI. However, when music became easily downloadable via the internet, the contribution in terms of value of such activity decreased dramatically.

Resources and competences

In order to develop a product which helps your customers do the job they want to get done, your decisions revolve around the **resources** and **competences** your organisation currently has, or can acquire, and how they can be exploited and combined for maximum advantage.

Resources are the *assets* the organisation possesses or can call upon from partners or suppliers. These may be tangible assets such as machinery or intangible ones such as brand, but they all represent inputs into a production process. **Competences** are the ways these assets are deployed. In other words, resources are what an organisation 'has' while competences represent what it 'does well'. Your ability to deliver a *unique* value proposition to your customers often relies on the **unique resources** you control but, more often, on the **core competences** of the organisation.

To be unique, an organisation's resources must be ones which are hard for its competitors to access or copy. A competence can be called **core** only when it involves activities and processes through which resources are deployed in such a way as to achieve a *competitive advantage* in ways that others cannot imitate or obtain. Unique resources might be the services of a great designer or exclusive access to an important raw material. A core competence could be the ability of an organisation's staff to work together and learn quickly from their mistakes or their capacity for innovative thinking. The resources and competences you need to acquire or develop are intimately linked to the value proposition you aim to offer.

How to identify unique resources and core competences

Having clarified what your *unique* value proposition is (or aims to be), it is crucial to identify what is needed, in terms of resources and competences, to successfully deliver it. Which of those resources and competences are the most important to drive your uniqueness towards competitors by giving you a sustainable competitive advantage? These are the unique resources and key competences you must have and nurture.

You should also objectively assess the strengths and weaknesses of the company's resources and capabilities.

By matching the two you might discover that you miss a key competence (for instance the capability to deliver on time if you are an online retailer) but you are extremely good at financial management).

To perform such an assessment, always start by **listing down what the key activities are** in order to deliver your value proposition. This allows you to confirm the unique resources and core competences you should master.

The second step is to look inside your organisation and to **list the assets** (both tangible and intangible) and **competences** your organisation has. For each item on this list you should ask two key questions:

1. How relevant is it to achieve my competitive advantage?
2. What is the relative position of the organisation (as compared to the other players)?

Use a **numerical scale** (for instance 1 to 10 where 5 would be 'average'). A maximum grade for both questions indicates a unique resource owned by the organisation (or a core competence) which represents one of its strengths (towards its competitors). By contrast, a competence with a high mark for question 1 but a low mark for question 2 indicates a serious weakness of the organisation (its competitors are better at mastering a core competence) so that reflection and action are required.

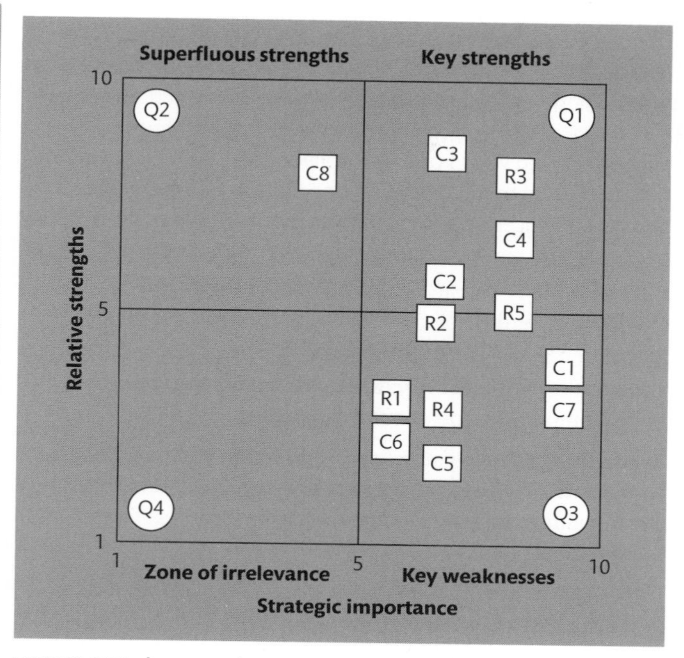

FIGURE 6.11 A competence–resource matrix

The results of this assessment can be effectively visualised through a simple matrix (see Figure 6.11) where C1 to C8 are the organisation's competences and R1 to R5 its resources.

- Quadrant Q1 presents all the unique resources and core competences the organisation already has.
- Q2 shows **superfluous strengths**. For these the challenge is to turn apparently irrelevant strengths into valuable resources and capabilities.
- All the resources and competences in Q3 represent the organisation's **key weaknesses**. Converting weakness into strength is likely to be a long-term task for most organisations and outsourcing may be a solution.
- Finally, Q4 is a **zone of irrelevance**.

Value network

No matter what product or service the company delivers, it will always need resources and competences from elsewhere and will ask other companies to perform certain activities. For instance, the company may rely on external suppliers for its raw materials, or may need external companies to review its accounts or distribute its products.

It is rare for an organisation to undertake internally all the value-creating activities from product design to delivery to the final customer. In most cases, companies are part of a wider value network. A **value network** (see Figure 6.12) is defined by Johnson and Whittington (*Fundamentals of Strategy*, Pearson Education, 2009) as'the set of inter-organisational links and relationships that are necessary to create a product or a service'.

As a manager, it is extremely important for you to analyse your value network. You need to think about how it could be managed more effectively or efficiently to deliver your value proposition to your target customers. For instance, if you produce televisions, the value you deliver to your customers is not only influenced by the set of activities that you undertake within your manufacturing company. You will probably buy components from external suppliers and distribute your products through independent electronics stores. Both the quality of the components and the customer service provided by your retailers will affect the value delivered to your customers.

Questions to ask about your value network include:

- Where are cost and value created? What costs do the different organisations or people in the network incur and what type of margins do they apply to their own products and services?

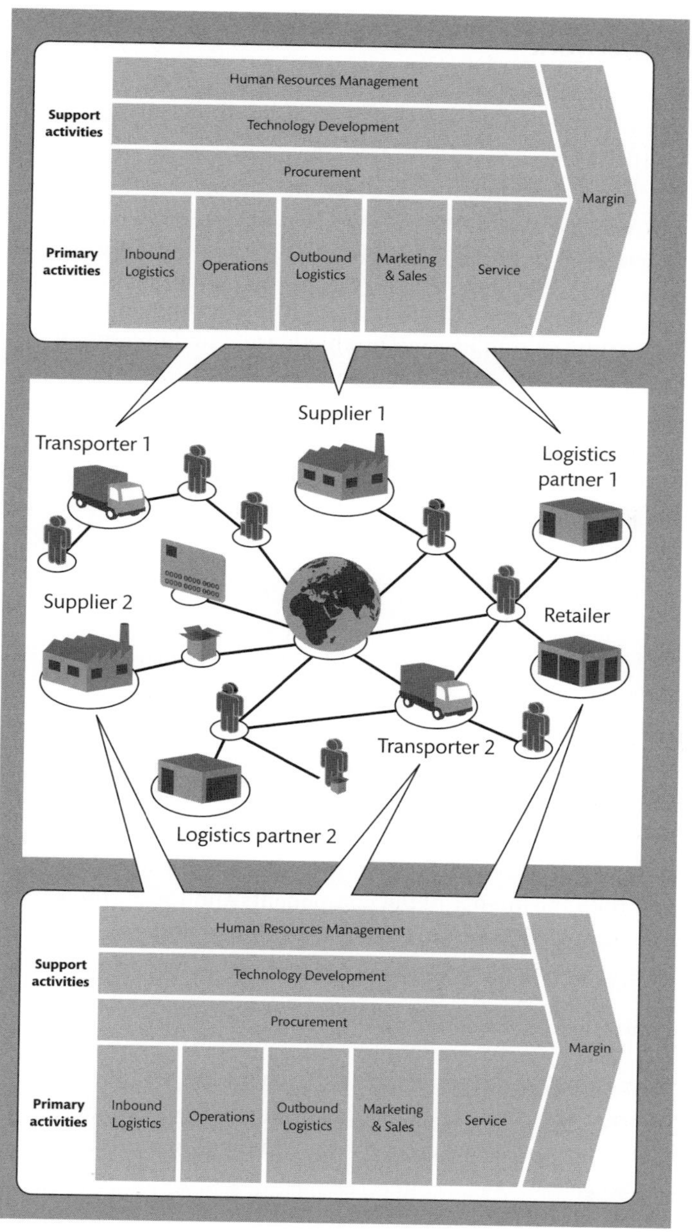

FIGURE 6.12 A typical value network

- Which activities are central to your own strategic capability and which are less crucial? In most circumstances it is advisable to retain direct control over the most important activities, especially where they relate directly to your core competences.
- Where are the profit pools? **Profit pools** refer to the different levels of profit available in different parts of the value network. Due to differences in competitive intensity, some parts of the value network might be structurally more profitable than others. For example, in the computer industry, microprocessors and software have traditionally been more profitable than hardware manufacture. Identifying the profit pools does not mean that the organisation has to automatically jump into them! You may lack the resources or competences needed to enter that field or the market may not recognise your firm as being credible in that area. For example, in the 1990s, many car manufacturers realised that greater potential profits were available in services such as car hire. However, they were not equipped to succeed in that market.
- Make or buy? The make or buy decision for a particular activity or component is critical. The more your organisation outsources, the more its ability to manage other organisations becomes a critically important competence in itself.
- Who might be the best partner in the various parts of the value network? There are likely to be a number of companies able to provide the service you require. Your choice will influence the success of your value proposition and therefore must be based on more than just cost.
- What kind of relationship should be developed with each partner? As the automotive industry has shown, many organisations have benefited from establishing closer relationships with suppliers, cooperating in activities such as R&D, design and market intelligence.

Remember that your product or service is only successful to the extent that it gets the job done for customers. It is unlikely that your organisation has, internally, all the competences and resources required to do this. Taking this point of view will force you to consider which relationships with which companies, perhaps even outside the conventional boundaries of your industry, should be developed in order to solve your customer's problem.

It is important to underline the tricky and complex relationship between your value network and your competitive environment. Since your direct competitors are those whose offerings are the closest to yours, they also share part or most of your value network. Your ability to manage this network effectively will put your organisation in a favourable or unfavourable position as compared to the competition. It is also worth noting that although the competitive environment and the value network are clearly separate in the CAES framework, in practice the boundaries between the two are much more flexible and permeable.

In some circumstances, your competitors might become part of your value network. Think about the agreement reached by Ford, Mercedes, Renault and Nissan to jointly develop the technology for hydrogen cars. In many circumstances, your distribution will rely on the distribution network of a competitor or you will buy a raw material from one of them.

Organisational culture

As discussed in Chapter 5, in the end your ability to implement your strategic initiatives and to successfully meet your clients' needs largely depends on the culture present within the organisation.

Regardless of the quality of your resources or the potential attractiveness of your value proposition to your target customers, the culture is the invisible hand that will make the different components of the system work harmoniously or crush them into chaos. This will of course have an impact on the relative cost and price the firm can achieve through its selected strategy. For example, a cost-leadership strategy will require everyone in the organisation to be very focused in eliminating unnecessary waste, requiring people to be very mindful and aligned in their behaviours.

The key messages of this chapter

- The first stage of the strategy development process aims to help you assess where you are and how your current strategy creates, or inhibits, competitive advantage. The CAES framework can be used for an in-depth understanding of many different elements, both within and outside the organisation, and their interrelationships.
- The macro-environmental factors that influence the performance of a business sector can be explored using the PESTEL framework. These factors can explain some of the variance in performance between different sectors, but for a fuller picture we need look at the forces at work within an industry, using Porter's five forces model.
- The internal analysis helps us analyse the main components of our business model and the way they interact to create competitive advantage. The cornerstone of any business model is the value proposition.
- Creating a product or a service involves carrying out a number of activities. These have to be scrutinised in order to understand how each activity contributes to value creation and at what cost. Porter's value chain model is very useful in understanding how value is created or lost in terms of the activities undertaken by the organisation.
- In order to develop a product which helps your customers do the job they want to get done, decisions revolve around

the competences and capabilities the organisation currently has, or can acquire, and how they can be exploited and combined for maximum advantage.

- Resources are the assets the organisation possesses or can call upon from partners or suppliers. These may be tangible or intangible but they all represent inputs into a production process. Competences are the ways these assets are deployed.
- No matter what product or service the organisation delivers, it will always need resources and competences from elsewhere and will ask other organisations to perform certain activities. In most cases, organisations are part of a wider value network.

ACTION POINTS

- Be curious and try to understand where superior value creation comes from, using the CAES framework. Focus on your business model and its configuration such as value proposition, positioning, key activities, etc. To begin with, define the boundaries of your industry in order to better understand in which court you play and who your competitors are.
- Have you ever thought of your core competences, the ones that make you unique and create a sustainable competitive advantage? A must-have exercise is to identify your core competences, understand to what extent they are really core, and reflecting on how you could extend your business by leveraging them.
- Take one day away from your normal routine and reflect with your team on your profitability and how it compares to your industry? Use PESTEL and the five forces model to figure out the critical factors that drive the profitability of your industry.

7 Identifying the core challenges

FROM CARRYING OUT A SITUATION ANALYSIS by using the CAES framework, you will have gathered a wealth of clues and insights about the company's business model and about the external macro-environment and industry structure. You should now have a good understanding of the organisation's resources and competences, especially those that are at the core of what you do well; the ones that set you apart and make your value proposition unique. You also have a good view of the macro-trends that might affect your industry as well as the industry key success factors. These very specific observations provide clues and insights that will help in the search for the core challenges.

The Servicom success

A few weeks after the Jasmin revolution in Tunisia, Davide had the chance to meet Majdi Zarkouna, the CEO of Servicom Group, a Tunisian company that is the epitome of a modern, well-run organisation. At first sight, Servicom looks like a dispersed conglomerate of unrelated businesses. It has a telecoms business that provides infrastructure services such as fibre optic cabling, switches and routers; plus a building equipment distribution and management business, including air conditioning and elevators. In terms of public works, Servicom constructs buildings and roads and also distributes mobile devices and office supplies. The company has enjoyed 30% plus annual growth since its inception in 2005 and it is now one of the stars on the Tunisian stock market with a market value six times higher than when its stock was first offered for sale in 2009.

Over a number of interesting discussions with Mr Zarkouna Davide learned how he could achieve such success in so short a time. He explained to Davide that all his businesses are project based and in sectors where the procurement is organised via tenders for public or private organisations. Winning one of these tenders depends on being able to meet demanding deadlines, comply with detailed administrative frameworks, correctly understand the brief and set very competitive prices. Many companies try to win tenders and fail. Others win but eventually lose money as a result of offering unrealistically low prices that do not cover their costs. In this challenging arena, Servicom wins tenders at double the average rate and has rarely lost a dinar (the local currency) in any project.

So what is Mr Zarkouna's secret? According to him, Servicom's success stems from a clear understanding of the company's core challenge: constructing a very efficient and effective workflow. This understanding came to Mr Zarkouna through the careful analysis of how different industry sectors function and through reviewing each and every project he had undertaken in his career. In response to this core challenge Mr Zarkouna has developed a unique competence in managing every single activity relating to a tender through a very structured process.

This process is automated using software specially developed in-house. This system, which is constantly being reviewed and updated, is the backbone of each Servicom's business. It allows Mr Zarkouna to monitor the whole process, from tender to submission of the proposal, and from the first purchase of material to the number of hours each employee works on the project. Understanding and then overcoming the core challenge of organising Servicom around the workflow system has put it in the enviable position of being the most competitive bidder but also the most profitable one.

How to identify challenges

Observations need to be organised. Some clues might be related to internal issues such specific brands, distribution channels, pricing, advertising or operational matters. Some might be about external factors such as the potential threat from new entrants, or the predicted decline of a customer segment that is important to the company. The best way to organise these observations is to classify them. This enables us to label the observations and put them in groups of related items. By doing this we can create order amongst the wide variety of observations that will have been generated about the company and its environment. This makes it easier to share them with other people in an easily understood format.

The labels we use will depend on the subject but if, for instance, we were observing a team at work we might have labels such as culture, communication, behaviour, outputs, relationships and processes. Labels like these, although overlapping, help to organise our thoughts. If we are observing customers we could classify them based on the total number of purchases in a year, or the frequency of their purchases, or the channel by which they purchase our products. For an online business, classifying customers by frequency of purchase is a quick way to build a useful picture of their customer base.

Knowing how many customers purchased once, twice, three times or more could trigger some useful questions. For example, if the majority of sales are coming from buyers who visit the site only once, this might suggest that the customer's experience of using the site is less than satisfactory.

One of the most commonly used classifications in business strategy is **SWOT**, which classifies the results of the situation analysis into strengths and weakness (from internal business model analysis) and opportunity and threats (from external analysis) – see Figure 7.1.

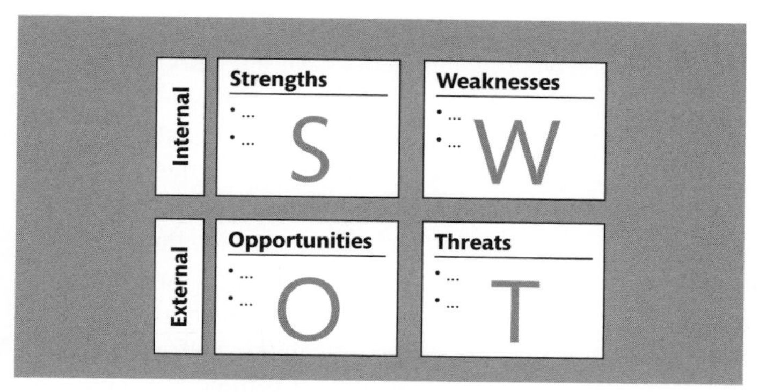

FIGURE 7.1 The SWOT framework

A note of caution about using SWOT

SWOT is a justifiably popular tool as it is simple to understand and practical to use. But however beautiful it may look, it remains just a matrix with four boxes. Its usefulness lies in its ability to summarise and draw together the information you have gathered through carrying out a robust examination of your situation. Without a thorough analysis, any SWOT is of little use. We sometimes hear managers say 'let's do a quick SWOT' when asked about the strategy of their department or business unit. This is clearly not the way to use it. SWOT's usefulness comes into play only after a thorough situation analysis has been done.

Classifications do help in the search for core challenges but their potential is limited. A much more powerful technique that builds on the outcome of classification is the identification of correlations. Correlations show us the links between different group of observations, allowing us to identify patterns and trends. Correlations can be powerful enough to make practical predictions about the future. For example, if elasticity (the extent to which demand is linked to price) is low and we increase prices then we can predict that revenues will go up.

Correlations are useful but present two challenges. The first is that even when we find apparently clear-cut correlations we may still suspect that it might simply be coincidence. This problem can be overcome through experimentation. By changing one variable and closely monitoring the others we discover whether or not the outcome is the one predicted by our correlation. So if we suspect that the improved performance of our staff is due to a certain training programme, we might want to test whether there really is a correlation by also tracking the performance of staff who have not had the training or who have been on a different course.

The second and more serious challenge is when we do not understand why the correlation exists. We are then haunted by the possibility that the correlation involves variables that we have not identified, or that we have not defined the known variables narrowly enough. The only way of overcoming this problem is to investigate cause and effect by applying root cause analysis.

A useful tool to establish correlations and identify potential core challenges is the TOWS matrix. This builds on the SWOT by applying the company's identified strengths and weaknesses to the threats and opportunities present in the external environment. It presents the company with the following questions:

- How could our strengths be used to take advantage of the opportunities we have identified?
- How could the opportunities be used to overcome our weaknesses?
- How could we use our strengths to overcome the threats we have identified?
- How can our weaknesses be minimised and threats avoided?

Figure 7.2 shows the application of the TOWS matrix to an animal health firm, generating a number of potential issues that the firm needs to address:

- By applying one of the company's strengths – its strong portfolio – to one of the opportunities – the growth of new channels such as supermarkets and online shopping – a potential challenge is identified: i.e. leveraging the strong portfolio through growing non-veterinary channels.
- By applying the company's strength in having a strong portfolio of brands to the threat of generic products, the challenge to further strengthen the brand among vets to fight the rise of generics can be identified.

	Strengths	**Weaknesses**
Opportunities	**SO challenges** ▪ Leverage strong portfolio through growing non-vet channels? ▪ Optimise price positioning in the vet channel? ▪ Commercialise product portfolio in countries where it is not?	**WO challenges** ▪ Reduce the number of SKUs and maximise price positioning on selected power and volume brands? ▪ Enter non-vet channels to leverage their increasing weight?
Threats	**ST challenges** ▪ Further strengthen strong brand image amongst vets to fight the rise of generics? ▪ Leverage strong brands to minimise discounts to distributors?	**WT challenges** ▪ Set up coordinated sales approach across the region, especially to cope with competition from generics. ▪ Train salesforce to introduce value-added services.

FIGURE 7.2 TOWS matrix for an animal health company

- By applying the fact that the salesforce is not recognised as a true partner (but rather as a supplier) to the threat represented by the loss of market share by veterinary practices, the potential challenge of how to train the salesforce to sell value-added services is created.
- Bringing together the identified weakness of having a huge number of stock-keeping units (SKUs) with the opportunity presented by the growth in several market segments.

By going through the disciplines of classifying our observations and then looking for, and testing, correlations, we can extract maximum value from the data available. But while these logic-based techniques provide good information, intuition can still play a key role. The ability to spot correlations or to come up with insights just by looking at groups of observations is greatly enhanced by expert intuition, which rapidly links the observations it sees with mental models formed out of previous experience. But intuition needs to be used with care as it can sometimes lead us to oversimplify issues or give too much weight to certain observations.

How to validate challenges

By using SWOT and TOWS to organise your insights and look for correlations, and drawing upon expert intuition, you will have identified several candidates for being your core challenges. Although these are strong possibilities, they are still just candidates awaiting final selection. Unless the real core challenges are identified, a company can fall into the trap of being busy doing things that will not really help. In order to validate and select the core challenges, the ones most worth pursuing, we need to remember what we have learned about the strategic-thinking process. In particular we need to apply the effect–cause–effect approach (see Figure 7.3).

This approach provides an effective way of separating effects from causes and distilling down our observations in order to

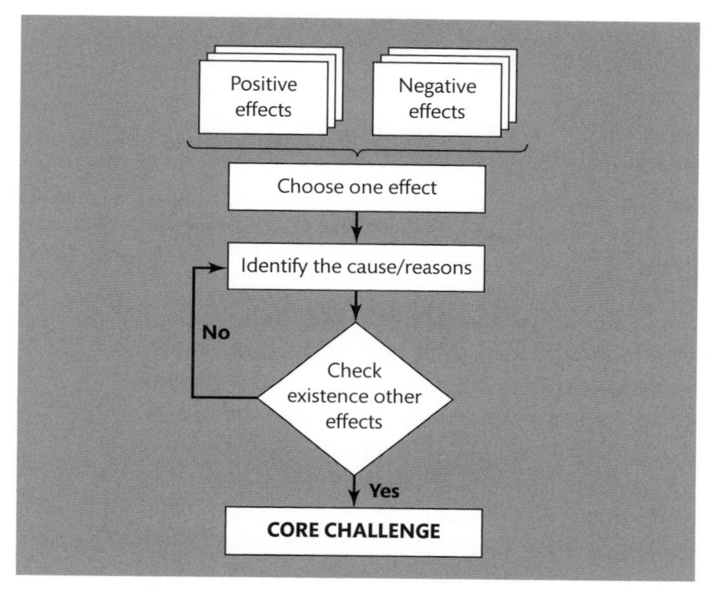

FIGURE 7.3 Effect–cause–effect approach

identify a core challenge. It is especially profitable to use this approach in a group setting, as the resulting consensus will be helpful in turning thoughts into coordinated action.

The effect–cause–effect method is also very powerful in terms of detecting biases or dogmas. A dogma is something that is held to be true and therefore beyond challenge. Dogmas can be found in organisational life as well as religion, where they serve as barriers to thinking and creativity. Our dogmas might lead us to rely, unthinkingly, on certain ways of recruiting and promoting staff or on a particular approach to marketing. Our trust in these methods may be misplaced but they are like articles of faith and are unlikely to be challenged.

Often when we have an unresolved core challenge, the reason is not our inability to tackle it, but our inability to even see it in the first place. Dogmas, habits, custom and practice and misplaced trust in people or procedures can create blind spots which prevent us from linking problems with their real, but hidden, causes. Using the effect–cause–effect approach will help us challenge dogmas and make clear links between cause and effect.

Using the effect–cause–effect method will help us to identify core challenges, but unfortunately not every challenge can be overcome. Investing time and resources in an impossible task cannot be considered a good strategy. So how do we work out whether the core challenge we have identified is potentially soluble? To do this we need to step back for a moment and think about the challenge and the wider issues that affect it (see Figure 7.4).

Figure 7.4 is a tool to assess the feasibility of addressing a core challenge. It forces us to consider:

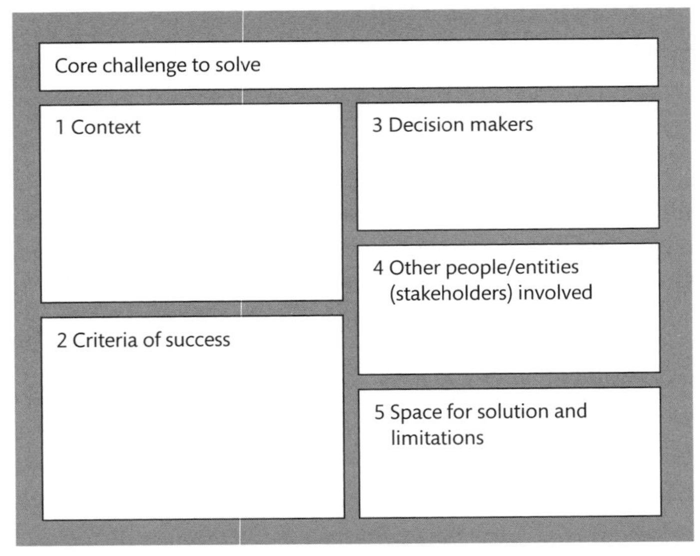

FIGURE 7.4 Core challenge definition

Source: based on McKinsey principles

- Who would be the stakeholders in the process of finding and implementing a solution? Who would be influential and who would be affected?
- What is the context of the challenge and what types of issues (e.g. technological, legal, organisational, etc.) must be considered?
- What constraints will we have to work with (e.g. time, resources, etc.)?
- What would constitute success?

Thinking through these issues will enable us to quickly evaluate whether it is worth pursuing a particular core challenge or if a different course of action would yield a better outcome. One of the most distinctive traits of the strategic mind is not so much the ability to solve the most complex core challenges, but rather the ability to identify the 'solvable' ones.

How to select core challenges – the importance of trade-offs

A commonly held mental model tells us that 'more is better'. This leads us to worry that if we do not do it all, we might leave out something crucial and miss an opportunity. Lots of companies keep generating new challenges, which are not necessarily core, that then become priorities. As a result, managers end up with a list of 10–20 top priorities! And when they ask which is the *real* priority they are told that each and every one is critically important. Of course, this is nonsense and a contradiction in terms. Once you have more than a very few priorities, they can no longer be priorities as they cannot all be given the required level of energy and focus.

The same applies when defining our core challenges: we tend to have too many. Why? There seems to be a natural tendency to pursue many challenges at the same time, perhaps in a search for multi-dimensional excellence, or simply in order to manage different stakeholders who have different ideas and priorities. Even when trying to reduce the number of core challenges to just the ones that absolutely need to be overcome, we still end up with too many.

What is the upper limit? It obviously depends on the complexity of the challenges you face but, as a rule of thumb, anything above what you can easily remember is too much. A memorable shortlist of challenges that staff throughout the organisation can easily recall will be more effective than endless lists of 'priorities', since it is more than likely that the organisation will lack the resources and focus to successfully address them all.

To keep the number of challenges low, we need to make trade-offs. As we discussed earlier, strategy is about choice, about deciding what to do but also what not to do. Creating a unique position in the market does not mean trying to do all that can possibly be done, and always offering more products and more services to even more segments. Rather, it is about making smart choices and focusing on what sets you apart.

Trade-offs are exclusive and each choice precludes or compromises the other. They can be viewed as forks on a road. Once you have taken one path, you cannot follow the other one. This might be obvious, but lots of companies seem unable to make real trade-offs. For instance, they try to top up their existing business model with that of the successful new player in the market.

The low-cost example

When facing the success of low-cost airlines like easyJet or Ryanair in the European market, Air France tried to replicate it by just adding a low-cost offer, Transavia, to its existing model. So far it has not been a particular success. For Air France, pursuing both a traditional and a low-cost model was like coming to a fork in the road and trying to go both ways at once.

> The Ryanair model is successful because it is based on avoiding a number of costly activities that Air France still carries out. For instance, Ryanair does not use airports in major cities and saves money by using ones situated in out-of-town locations. It is also successful because it has a strong culture, the invisible hand, which is not easily replicable.

In order to reduce the number of core challenges and select only those with the highest priority, which need immediate focus and which have a real chance of being overcome, three screening tests can be applied:

1. **Value creation:** will the core challenge significantly contribute to the creation of value for the organisation if it is overcome? Alternatively, will not addressing it lead to major value destruction?
2. **Resources and capabilities:** do we have the right resources and capabilities to address the core challenge?
3. **The invisible hand:** will the organisational culture assist in overcoming the core challenge or will it get in the way?

Subjecting potential core challenges to these three reality checks will help you choose ones that can be successfully tackled, and which are worth the time and energy required.

The value creation test is really about making the right trade-offs amongst the core challenges from a value perspective. This is critical in order to counterbalance our natural expert intuition that might push us to unconsciously favour challenges for which we have a particular affinity. A newly appointed head of a company, whose background is in R&D, might lean towards focusing on challenges that have an R&D component. Alternatively, someone promoted to CEO from the sales department might resist accepting that any challenges might be the result of poor performance by his former department.

Looking objectively at the real value that the core challenge will deliver in the short, medium and long terms is therefore paramount in making sure that we focus on that which creates maximum impact. A good proxy for this is the expected contribution to future profits. Our animal health company understood that not being present in distribution channels other than vets would ultimately mean closing itself off to half of the overall market within the next five years, as non-vet channels already represented 20% of the market and were growing quickly.

The next step is to consider whether we have the right resources and the necessary capabilities.

Improving customer relationships

A company we recently advised wanted to improve its customer relationships. Business customers were complaining that the client's focus was too short term and commercially driven, rather than based on the promotion of longer-term, mutually profitable partnerships. In response, the company developed a benchmarking tool for staff to support and enrich their discussions with customers. The tool gave useful insights to the customers about their current performance compared to their peers in the region and also provided suggestions for improvement.

The feedback from a small-scale experiment was excellent, with high levels of buy-in from staff and customers. This solution also met the core challenge of improving the quality of relationships with the company's most important business customers. However, due to a lack of focus, the company never managed to roll out the initial pilot successfully. On the one hand, sales resources were stretched too thinly by the simultaneous launch of three new products and the company's IT systems turned out to be incompatible with the new development and too rigid to change. Lack of resources, poor systems and an inability to make trade-offs got in the way of correctly addressing this core challenge.

This kind of situation happens frequently. Many projects, with a so-called top priority label, are handed over to extremely busy

> managers, who are asked to lead a new initiative in addition to their existing commitments. This approach seems to assume that the company is overstaffed with idle managers just waiting for more work.

Last but not least, the invisible hand of culture plays a major role in determining your success in addressing a core challenge. For instance, organisations where thinking outside the box is not permitted tend to kill initiatives in the womb. (No company will say that it does not want fresh thinking, but many make it abundantly clear through the example set by their top managers.) These initiatives might be critically needed to address the core challenge of an obsolescent business model which needs a radical overhaul.

Other organisations might say that they welcome new ideas, but punish mistakes harshly. In such companies, a mistake is a failure, and will be punished by the system. Needless to say, managers quickly realise that risk taking, even calculated risk taking, is not encouraged. This means that whatever the official line is, these companies do not want innovation, as risk and trial and error are part and parcel of the innovation process.

Defining what success will look like – strategic objectives and strategic guidelines

Now that we have a manageable number of core challenges to focus on, we need to establish what success will look like: in other words how the world is going to look if we overcome the identified challenges. To establish whether the core challenges are being successfully addressed, it is vital to define two elements: **strategic objectives** and **strategic guidelines**.

Strategic objectives

These take the form of one or few specific metrics and targets, defined for each core challenge. The metric and the targets should clearly show the progress towards overcoming the challenge, just as a target body weight will show your progress towards your target racing weight for the marathon you planned to run for your 40th birthday. The entire organisation will then feel comfortable that, if the targets are met, the core challenges have been successfully overcome.

Note that the metrics and the target defined here, which are referred to as strategic objectives, are a by-product of strategy, not the strategy itself. Defining a strategy is not about setting strategic objectives. It is primarily about identifying the right core challenges. The strategic objectives will follow as a consequence.

Often it is not possible to condense the overcoming of a core challenge into a single objective. Therefore each challenge may comprise one or more objectives, or goals, over a given period. These objectives must have the following characteristics:

- **Have a clear timeframe (2–5 years).** Saying when things need to happen can create a useful sense of urgency. The timeframe will depend on the context and the type of industry. For instance, five years is a normal strategic horizon for an established company in a stable market. On the other hand, for a high-tech company struggling to meet shareholder expectations, a 2–5 year horizon might seem a little too relaxed!
- **Be easy to understand and communicate at all levels of the organisation.** The strategic objectives should flow from a vision of the organisation which is widely shared throughout its workforce. If employees are unclear as a result of woolly thinking or too much jargon, objectives will be hard to communicate and implementation will be threatened.

- **Be challenging but achievable.** There is no point in having objectives that are not challenging. That is merely business as usual. Easily achieved objectives are unlikely to keep the company ahead of its competitors and sustain competitive advantage. On the other hand, objectives that are obviously beyond the reach of the company will just breed despondency and cynicism. The term 'stretch objectives' is a useful one to remember. The company needs to be challenged, but not to breaking point.
- **Have a clear impact on competitive advantage.** Strategic objectives must put the company in a position which enables it to achieve sustainable competitive advantage. The objectives must directly or indirectly ultimately impact either the relative price or the relative cost position of the firm. Failure to achieve such impact means that the strategic objective is not strategic at all.

The Poste Italiane example

An excellent example of how a well-designed strategic objective can support change is provided by the experience of Corrado Passera at the Italian Post Office, Poste Italiane. When he took over as MD, Poste Italiane was in a very sorry state. Its operations were inefficient and its productivity was amongst the lowest in the world. In addition, a huge number of complaints were being received about lost letters and packages.

Passera spent his first days examining the situation and personally visiting the organisation's facilities around Italy, including many post offices. He quickly realised that the core challenge was the supply chain, which to one degree or another included every single employee. He wanted to find a way to enable every member of staff to feel that they could help overcome this challenge and he also wanted a simple way for everyone to monitor progress.

Passera's solution was to set the objective of reducing the time it took to serve a customer during peak time from over 30 minutes to less than 10 minutes within three years. This clear strategic objective was simple, challenging and easy to monitor and, most importantly, everyone in the business could see how they could contribute to achieving it. The postman could see that by delivering packages correctly less people would need go to the post office. The office workers could see that by being properly trained and by using adequate technology they could increase the speed of service. Executives could now evaluate any investment proposition by looking at how much it would help to reduce queues at post offices. In fact all employees, and even suppliers and other stakeholders, were encouraged to suggest improvements as long as they would contribute to the achievement of the target.

The results were staggering. Within 24 months Poste Italiane had reduced average queuing time in most offices to less than five minutes, exceeding its target. This allowed it to reach profitability and invest in new activities such as banking, insurance and other logistic services using the resources freed up by its improved supply chain.

Strategic guidelines

As well as defining strategic objectives for each core challenge, the other vital task is to draw up strategic guidelines. Strategic guidelines define the boundaries of what can be done and what cannot be done, including any constraints that the organisation needs to take into account in achieving the strategic goals and overcoming the core challenge. In other words, they define the solution space within which initiatives can be developed.

Strategic guidelines help to verbalise and visualise the type of changes that need to occur and provide overall direction for the many actions which will be needed for strategic change. They cover 'soft' as well as 'hard' core challenges; culture and attitudes as well as systems and processes. Strategic guidelines are the highest level of strategy and, consequently, are normally developed at board level.

A very simple technique that can be used to communicate strategic guidelines is the **From–To framework**. The 'From' represent the core challenges and the 'To' is the desired outcome that will result from overcoming them.

Renault's strategic guidelines

When Carlos Ghosn, the current CEO, took the helm at Renault, the carmaker was not in an ideal situation. The company was losing money and its line-up of models was in drastic need of an update with only one new model, the Laguna, in the pipeline. On the basis of a situation analysis, Carlos and his new management team set out their strategic guidelines in the form of a From–To framework. The five bullet points under the 'From' heading were the five major challenges faced by the company (see Figure 7.5).

These guidelines have led to the creation of a much stronger company which today is a world leader in at least two segments of the car market; low-cost cars and fully electric cars.

From . . .	To . . .
A French-centred culture and organisation	A cross-cultural and decentralised organisation leveraging an alliance with Nissan
A management rewarded on sales volume achievement	Rewards on profits
A management by function and cost centre	A management by programmes
Voitures à vivre (cars to enjoy)	*Voitures à vendre* (cars that sell)
Long-term targets (14 million vehicles in 2010)	Medium-term commitments (3.3 million vehicles in 2005)

FIGURE 7.5 Renault's strategic guidelines in the early 2000s

Source: Renault's CEO's interview in *Les Echos* (2004)

Developing a From–To framework is a good way to ensure a team is correctly aligned around the core challenges, with everyone sharing a view of what is strategically important for the business. A great deal of time and energy will be dissipated if team members are moving in slightly different, or even opposite, directions. To achieve synergy, where the team becomes more than the sum of its parts, there must be a deep and genuine agreement between members about priorities and focus.

Companies that understand the value of team synergy might use the From–To framework at an off-site event and ask the team to work together to agree five statements that summarise the business's current situation in terms of core challenges, as in the example above. Then, the team would work on five statements that best describe where they would like the business to be in 3–5 years' time, once the core challenges have been successfully tackled.

The key messages of this chapter

- The basis of good strategic objectives is a thorough situation analysis of the company and the environment in which it operates.
- Identifying the core challenges and selecting the right goals to address them is probably the manager's most important responsibility. Core challenges might be external or internal.
- The SWOT framework is a helpful (but not exclusive) way of organising and presenting the main points, typically clues and insights from a situation analysis.
- The potential core challenges arising from organising the clues and insights need to be validated. Intuition is useful in this context but needs to be balanced by more objective techniques such as correlation using the TOWS framework and the effect–cause–effect approach.

- It is a mistake to try to pursue too many challenges. Trade-offs must be made or the success of strategic initiatives may be threatened by compromise.
- Challenges must also be assessed in terms of their likely contribution to value creation and the feasibility of tracking them successfully, given the resources and capabilities the company possesses.
- Strategic guidelines, in the form of the From–To framework, provide high-level context and guidance for strategic actions. These guidelines must be based on a shared understanding of the company's current position and desired direction of travel.
- Metrics must be selected that will enable management to discern progress towards overcoming the core challenges. These will be a set of specific targets directly linked to core challenges. These targets must be stretching but achievable, have clear time frames, be easy to communicate, and guarantee financial results.

ACTION POINTS

- Assemble and consolidate all the observations and insights you gathered in the situation analysis, and organise them using the SWOT framework. Pick one of the observations and apply the effect–cause–effect approach. Once you found a cause, pick another observation and see if you can justify it with the previously found cause. Repeat a few times. Once you have found a cause that justifies several effects then you know you have a core challenge.
- Do not pursue all core challenges but choose only a few to address, with a three-level screening: contribution to value creation, resources and capabilities needed, and alignment to the invisible hand of your organisation.
- With strategic objectives, define what success would look like when the core challenges are successfully overcome.

Your strategic objectives should take the form of one or few specific metrics and targets, defined for each core challenge. Be challenging but realistic!

- Use a From–To framework to define your strategic guidelines. This will help to verbalise and visualise the type of changes that need to occur. They will also provide overall direction for the many actions which will be needed to address the core challenges. A From–To framework is also an efficient tool to get the team to converge and agree on what the situation is today and where the organisation should be going.

8 Solving the core challenges

ONCE YOU HAVE DETERMINED YOUR CORE CHALLENGES and used these to set your goals, the next question to address is how they can be overcome. Which strategic initiatives and which solutions should be developed in order to address the core challenges? On which activities should the organisation focus? Obviously intuition can help here, especially when it comes from an experienced and successful manager. In Chapter 2 the senior consultant solved the challenge of the cash-strapped airline very simply: he used his experience gained over the years to decide that the only correct solution was to immediately increase prices by 20%. And because his intuition was good, this solution worked. However, not everybody has the talent and years of experience that lead to such accurate, intuitive judgements.

The good news is that, even if such excellent intuition is unavailable, there are practical approaches and frameworks that you can use to generate effective strategic initiatives. The example below shows how the problem of constructing a bread-making machine was overcome thanks to what is referred to as the 'solution shop' approach. This way of tackling problems combines the skills and knowledge of different people to create fresh perspectives and helps expose the biases that are often present when a problem has been around for a long time.

A breakthrough product

When, in the mid-1980s, the Japanese firm Matsushita decided to develop a domestic bread-making machine, one of the early problems it encountered was how to mechanise the process of kneading the dough. It was trying to replicate a skill which takes master bakers years to perfect and, initially, it encountered failure after failure. Eventually a member of the development team, Ikuko Tanaka, decided to volunteer to become an apprentice of the head baker at the Osaka International Hotel. In observing and trying to copy his technique, she noticed that he both stretched and twisted the dough in a particular way.

Matsushita then assembled a team that spanned specialisms and professional cultures, including product planning, engineering, software development and control systems, to replicate this 'twisting stretch' motion. After a year of experimentation, with each trial building on the lessons of the last, a successful prototype was built. Its success depended on the way the different team members combined their experience and expertise and worked closely together. For example, the engineers redesigned the dough case to hold the dough better as it was churned, and another team member suggested delaying the addition of the yeast to prevent over-fermentation.

This story provokes several questions. How did Tanaka spot the critical aspect of the baker's technique, and how was she able to link it to the design challenge she faced? Also, how did so many different types of expertise and intelligence combine to produce such a marvellous new product?

Reducing the complexity of the core challenge

Core challenges are by nature not easy to solve. If they were, they would not be core challenges. They may have multiple aspects, including social, economic, legal and technological. Their solution may require numerous types of processes and activities such as modelling and market testing. They also require a good understanding of how the different core challenges interrelate and influence each other. The first step in tackling a core challenge is therefore to **reduce its complexity** by identifying its core components and breaking it down into several simpler problems.

Identifying the key constituents of the core challenge

Logic trees (sometimes called issue trees) are particularly helpful in using logic to break a core challenge down into its constituent parts. Looked at vertically, the logic tree separates the issue into its various components, while reading it from left to right adds progressively more and more detail (see Figure 8.1).

Logic trees are useful in identifying potential solutions in two ways:

1. Solutions can be derived by breaking down the core challenge using a series of 'how' questions and identifying all the possible alternatives to fix the problem.
2. The validity and quality of the identified solutions can be quickly tested by using a logic tree to argue why a solution should be considered.

To be effective, a logic tree needs to provide an insightful breakdown and obey three basic rules:

- **Relevance:** the elements of any level (reading vertically) must be both sufficient and necessary to support the preceding level by consistently answering a 'why' or a 'how' question; progressing from the key question or problem to the analysis as it moves from left to right.
- **Coherence:** elements of the same level must have the same nature.

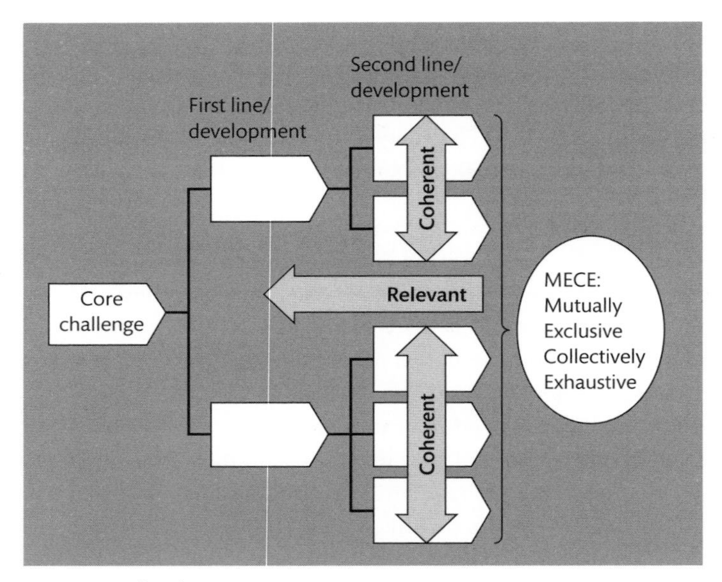

FIGURE 8.1 Logic tree structure

Source: based on McKinsey principles

- **MECEness**: the branches must be mutually exclusive and collectively exhaustive, i.e. the elements must be independent and together they must represent the whole problem. According to the mutually exclusiveness principle, the branches of the logic tree should 'exclude' each other and be distinct. While collectively exhaustiveness refers to the idea that the branches should 'exhaust' the relevant field.

Logic trees are commonly used when starting the problem-solving process from scratch, when there is no other obvious framework to use and no appropriate mental model to draw upon. Most core challenges are unique, and therefore building a logic tree helps by encouraging fresh thinking as opposed to trying to use a model intended for a different sort of situation. Another advantage of logic trees is that, used properly, they bring the re-assurance that the route to a solution lies somewhere within the branches.

Figure 8.2 shows the issue of a manufacturing site that needs to considerably reduce its energy costs. We can see that the tree is logical, relevant, coherent and MECE. We also feel confident that the core challenge is broken down into simpler constituents, each of them being part of the solution.

Another excellent way of breaking down a core challenge into manageable parts is **mind mapping** which graphically represents all the components of an issue and how they interrelate. A mind map starts with a word or phrase which summarises the core challenge placed in a circle or box in the centre of a blank piece of paper. The main sub-challenges, ideas or issues are placed in circles radiating from the core challenge and joined to it by a line. These in turn can be linked to their own sub-challenges or ideas. Issues that are related in some way can be linked by drawing a line between them. There are many mind mapping images and related software on the web (e.g. http://www.tonybuzan.com).

By laying out all the salient points on a single piece of paper and figuring out how they may impact on one another, using a mind map can promote a more holistic, 360-degree view of a core challenge. It also avoids the errors that purely linear thinking sometimes leads to. Just as importantly, this technique allows several people to work together and add to each other's understanding as they create the map.

Understanding the importance of its constituents

By breaking down a core challenge we make finding a solution simpler, but not necessarily simple. In most cases, the solution is likely to lie in a combination of approaches, not in one single 'silver bullet' answer. In the logic tree concerned with reducing energy bills, it is clear that each of the small branches represents a lever for reducing costs, but no single one of them will, by itself, drastically lower the energy bill. Yet not all branches are of the same importance.

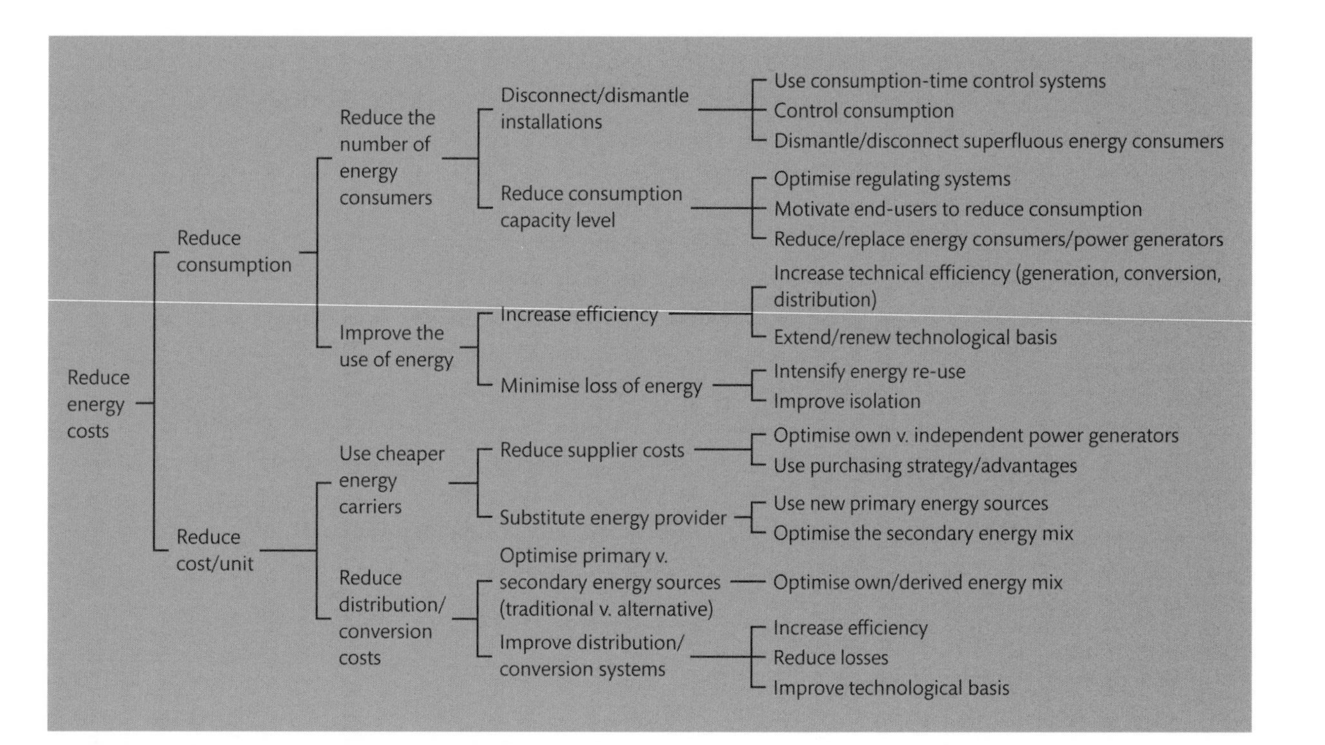

FIGURE 8.2 Logic tree to reduce a site energy bill

Source: based on McKinsey principles

Reducing the consumption (the upper first-level branch) is a key constituent and should be addressed no matter what. However, focusing only on the lower, unit-cost branch will not necessarily lead to a lowering of cost. There is no guarantee that a cheaper supplier will be found or that the benefits offered by the new supplier will be anything other than a short-term measure designed to attract new customers.

Understanding the relative importance of the core constituents is vital in successfully addressing the core challenge. Overlooking or neglecting one or more of the main constituents will lead to a flawed solution.

A simple way to understand and represent the relative importance of the various components is to assign a weighting to each one. This could be the product of a scientific analysis, expert opinion or just your best guess based on the information available. The weighting system could be numerical (e.g. each component is given a score between 1 and 10, where 10 = critical for success) or qualitative (e.g. components are categorised as either essential or desirable).

Reducing complexity leads to a clearer understanding about which of the constituents should become the focus in the search for solutions.

Developing potential solutions

Having reduced the complexity of the core challenge we can begin to look for a solution to the core challenge that faces the business. The solution will always be something which is novel; either fresh new thinking, a reworking or a clever combination of existing ideas. Therefore one of the essential ingredients for developing solutions must be creativity, by which we mean the ability to connect existing mental models to form new ones. Steve Jobs called this joining the dots, where new connections are made between ideas, techniques or facts previously seen as separate. There are many ways of stimulating creativity, but we will focus on three in particular: lateral thinking, the solution shop approach and co-creation workshops.

Lateral thinking

Tackling a core challenge is not a mechanical process. Logic trees and mind maps are helpful in simplifying the issue, but intuition and imagination will get you nearer to a solution. And imagination is not just a matter of luck. One of its enablers is curiosity. People who come up with disruptive, out-of-the-box, ideas tend to be curious by nature. They read a lot, mix with people from different backgrounds and accumulate information from all over the place. They are then able to 'connect the dots' between seemingly unrelated ideas and facts to create new ideas. In other words, they are good lateral thinkers.

The term lateral thinking was coined by Edward de Bono who explored the power of unconventional thinking. Conventional thinking is vertical; reductionist in nature, it seeks to critique possible ways forward and discard all but the right one. Creative thinking is lateral; it seeks richness of ideas more than rightness, it explores all possible angles on an issue in order to generate many solutions. Whereas vertical thinking is sequential and analytical, lateral thinking can move in leaps and is provocative, challenging conventional wisdom. Where vertical thinking approaches issues in a direct, logical, step-by-step way, lateral thinking comes at issues sideways, exploiting ideas and knowledge from every source and joining the dots in unpredictable ways to solve the puzzle.

Lateral thinking takes different forms in different industries.

Lateral thinking examples

Netflix on demand

When telecom or cable companies such as Verizon or Comcast were considering their future strategy, a move into supplying customers with content (e. g. movies) must have seemed tempting, not least as it would prevent these companies from becoming mere suppliers of bandwidth. This could be done via the connections they already had into customers' homes to provide internet and TV.

This might look like out-of-the-box thinking but it was unfortunately not good enough. Further lateral thinking would have led them to identify the threat posed by the likes of Netflix and Lovefilm (part of Amazon). Netflix came up with a business model that could stream movies and TV programmes on demand not only to cable or internet-connected TVs but also computers and game consoles. And rather than requiring customers to pay for each movie, it offered unlimited content for a small monthly fee.

In comparison to this all-you-can-eat access to a huge menu of content, the pay-per-view offerings of most telecoms companies look decidedly less appetising.

Xerox and its service line

People who regard Xerox as a printer company might have been surprised by a recent series of advertisements. The campaign highlights the services Xerox provides to some of its high-profile business clients. 'We focus on managing Virgin America's call centres. So they don't have to' boasts one ad. Another announces that 'We focus on digitising P&Gs documents worldwide. So they don't have to'. Other prestigious clients mentioned include Ducati and Marriott. But what has providing business services got to do with printers? And how did Xerox connect the dots to make what seems like such a bold move?

First note an important clue. For a long time Xerox has defined itself not as a manufacturer of printers but as 'The Document

Company'. Rather than just selling printers, Xerox provided printing solutions for its clients. And as a provider of solutions, it established good relationships with businesses and built up a much better and broader understanding of their needs regarding not just printing but document management in general. With a firm foothold in document-related business services, Xerox went further, leveraging its own expertise at running printer repair call centres to offer call centre services to their clients.

Thinking widely and creatively opened up opportunities that conventional, tramline thinking would not have seen.

Solution shop approach

In his book *The Innovator's Prescription* (McGraw Hill Professional, 2008), Harvard Business School professor and innovation guru Clayton Christensen develops the concept of a solution shop for hospitals. Solution shops are a technique for diagnosing and solving complex, unstructured problems.

A general hospital's solution shop is designed to diagnose patients' problems regardless of where they occur. To achieve this, the hospital should have at least one physician of every speciality having at their disposal a wide range of diagnostic equipment. The physicians and available equipment should be separated and not linked by any standardised processes to give the specialists the necessary freedom of action to accomplish the desired outcomes.

The Mayo Clinic

The Mayo Clinic is organised in solution shops. Physicians, equipment and processes are organised in a way that mirrors the human organ system in order to deliver diagnoses in a quick and cost-effective way. The executive check-up solution targets executives and offers them a fast, reliable and comprehensive check-up. It includes services such as a comprehensive medical history and physical examination by specialists in internal and preventive medicine, a full range of preventive screening tests

> for early detection of cancer, heart disease and other serious medical problems, a cardiovascular fitness evaluation, including a treadmill exercise test and an exercise prescription, a lifestyle assessment to discuss nutrition, stress management, alcohol, tobacco, personal safety and other indicators of risk of disease, as well as a review and update of medications and immunisations, including those needed for international travel. A full report of the test results at the conclusion of the examination and a written report are sent to the executive's home.

In the same way that the Mayo Clinic has re-organised itself into solution shops to serve its patients, any organisation could use this approach to help its customers find answers to the problems they face. Specialists and experts with different skills could explore the customers' situation from a variety of perspectives and offer their 'diagnosis' and recommend a 'treatment'.

Co-creation workshops

Co-creation is a relatively new marketing approach that has revolutionised the way firms interact with their customers and stakeholders in general. Instead of treating consumers as passive recipients of a service, co-creation encourages the active involvement of customers in the value chain of the company by integrating their knowledge, experience and creativity in the development of products and services.

C. K. Prahalad and Venkat Ramaswamy developed the concept of co-creation in their book *The Future of Competition* (Harvard Business Review Press, 2004). According to the two scholars, customers are becoming more and more co-creaters of value rather than simple recipients of products or services.

Many companies have adopted the concept of co-creation and the trend has accelerated in the past few years.

Co-creation examples

Nordstrom, the American retailer of clothing, shoes and accessories, used co-creation to develop an iPad app for sunglasses in just a week. The customers visiting their Seattle flagship store were involved in the testing process of the different prototypes and provided feedback at each step of the production process.

Coca-Cola has also used co-creation in the development of a marketing campaign named 'Energising refreshment', where customers' ideas were used in advertisements.

Tannish, the jewellery arm of the Tata Group, used co-creation in the form of a contest named 'My expression' where customers were invited to submit ideas for jewellery for one of the company's collections. The winner was given the opportunity to collaborate with a designer to produce pieces of jewellery for the company and the other finalists received large cash prizes.

Practical tools for generating solutions

Having shared a few approaches that can help stimulate creativity, we now turn to two highly effective 'solution generator' tools.

The blue ocean strategy

Developed by the academics Kim and Mauborgne at the turn of the century, the blue ocean approach is based on the view that market boundaries and industry structure are not fixed. Instead of treating the nature of the market or industry as a given, the blue ocean view is that industry players can reconstruct it, not through competition but by creating a new market where there are no competitors. The competition therefore becomes irrelevant.

Figure 8.3 shows the main characteristics of blue ocean strategy and contrasts it with red ocean strategy, where

Blue ocean	Red ocean
Create uncontested market space	Compete in existing market space
Make the competition irrelevant	Beat the competition
Create and capture new demand	Exploit existing demand
Break the value/cost trade-off	Make the value/cost trade-off
Align the whole system of a company's activities in pursuit of differentiation and low cost	Align the whole system of a company's activities with its strategic choice of differentiation or low cost
Set up the rules of 'the game'	Accept existing rules of 'the game'

FIGURE 8.3 Blue ocean v. Red ('bloody') ocean

Source: Chan, K. W. and Mauborgne R. (2005) *Blue Ocean Strategy: How to Create Uncontested Market Space and Make Competition Irrelevant*, Harvard Business Press, p.5, October 2004. Copyright © 2005 by the Harvard Business School Publishing Corporation, all rights reserved, reprinted by permission of Harvard Business School.

companies compete for space in a crowded market. The blue ocean approach taps into latent demand to extend the frontiers of the industry or even create a new industry by providing entirely new products or addressing new market segments in a way that cannot be easily replicated by competitors. The company can therefore create its own market space, making the competition irrelevant and setting the rules of the game. Obviously, at some stage, competitors will try to cash in on the newly created market but by then it may be too difficult or too late.

There are two ways to create a Blue Ocean: by launching completely new industries (e.g. eBay and online auctions) or by creating a blue ocean from within a red ocean, when a company expands the boundaries of an existing industry. In most cases companies use the second way by trying to address latent demand.

How do you create a blue ocean from a red one? Organisations who have done this successfully have been prepared to abandon or change products and ways of working and invent new ones. As a start, try to identify the features of the product or service around which most players in your market compete in the conventional red ocean. Then, explore where latent, unmet demand might lie and focus on the features that are important to this group of potential customers. The product can then be deconstructed and rebuilt around these features. You might need to introduce features that would be irrelevant in a red ocean, but these could be the factors that open up a new, blue ocean space for your company.

At the core of the blue ocean is the *eliminate-reduce-raise-create framework*. This poses questions that can lead to a radical rethink of a product:

- Which features should be **eliminated** because they are not creating any value in the blue ocean?
- Which features should be **reduced** because they no longer make the product stand out from its competitors?
- Which features should be **increased** or even **created** because they are valued highly by blue ocean customers?

Many best-practice organisations have used blue ocean strategy, sometimes without knowing it. The Indian company Murugappa transformed its business and changed the structure of an industry using a blue ocean approach.

A blue ocean strategy story: the Murugappa Group

The context

Founded in 1900, the Murugappa Group is one of India's leading business conglomerates with a turnover of more than $4 billion. The group has 28 businesses including eight listed companies, and is a market leader in several industries: abrasives, car components, cycles, sugar, fertilizers, plantations, bioproducts and nutraceuticals.

The core challenge

Murugappa wanted to turnaround its loss-making fertiliser business, Coromandel International. It decided to look for a strategy that could outperform the competition but not by creating a cost advantage or perfecting the product. Instead, it planned to create a blue ocean and make the competition irrelevant.

The fertiliser business is subsidy-driven, with no rewards for innovation and no incentive to invest in technology. The key questions for Murugappa were:

- How can we win customers, and offer an innovative value proposition?
- How can we innovate new products, and create something that could be profitable without being subsidised?
- How can we find new, currently unused, sources for the products?

The value created

The company invested in innovation and created a new business model, which delivered:

- new services, by creating a retail chain of 500 full-service centres that sold products and services to farmers;
- a new source for its products, by turning municipal waste into compost;
- new products with augmented convenience, by setting up two soluble fertiliser units, a non-subsidy source of revenue.

In the process of creating its blue ocean, the company has developed much closer links with farmers. It has also expanded globally, setting up a phosphoric acid business and consultancy service. At the start of the process, the fertiliser company's shares were trading at Rs 40; today they trade at Rs 240.

Creating a blue ocean

Murugappa succeeded by creating a blue ocean. Its actions can be summarised using the *eliminate-reduce-raise-create* framework:

- **Eliminate.** No specific activity was radically eliminated.
- **Reduce.** Its dependence on subsidies was reduced by setting up two soluble fertiliser units, a source of revenue that was not dependent on subsidy.
- **Raise.** The product mix developed and a complete plant nutrition solutions company, with organic fertilizers, specialty nutrients and compost produced from municipal waste resulted.
- **Create.** A service and retail business, involving more than 420 rural retail centres was created.

The seven degrees of freedom

Another popular framework for generating potential solutions is the '**seven degrees of freedom**'. The tool is adapted to the core challenges of top-line growth, when a steep and sustainable increase of sales is needed. Typical situations occur when rising competition leads to declining market share or lower prices, when achieving economies of scale has become necessary to remain competitive, or when playing on a global scale is a must.

It consists of a ladder with seven steps, with the steps becoming bolder and more radical as you climb higher (see Figure 8.4). The first step is to think about what can be improved within the scope of existing products and existing customers. Step two unleashes an extra degree of freedom, focusing on reaching out to new customer segments with existing products (or services). The next step opens up the possibility of modifying products or launching new ones for both existing and new customers. Step 4 opens up greater degrees of freedom in terms of new ways to deliver, new

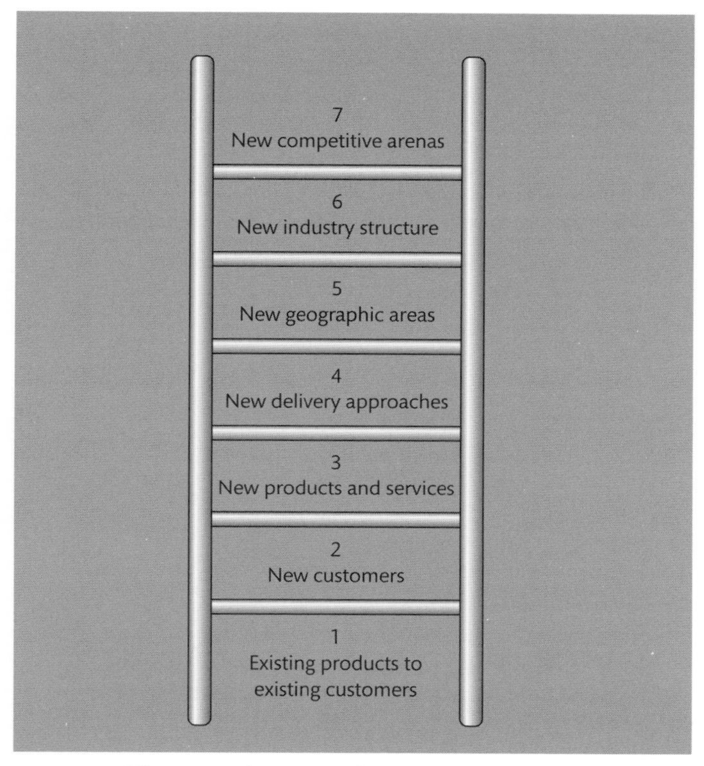

FIGURE 8.4 The seven degrees of freedom ladder

Source: adapted from Baghai, M. , Coley, S. and White, D. (2000) *The Alchemy of Growth: Practical Insights for Building the Enduring Enterprise*, Perseus Books Group

territories, changing the industry structure through strategic alliances, mergers or acquisitions, and eventually considering moving into completely new competitive arenas.

This framework is a good way of stimulating ideas for potential solutions, and winning strategies can be built from all seven degrees of freedom. It can easily be used as the structure for a workshop or time-out, where teams could be asked to focus on one level in particular or challenged to come up with several ideas from each level.

Questions to ask at each level

1. **Existing products to existing customers.** This is about trying to tap in the potential of existing clients with your existing portfolio of products.
   - How could we increase sales to existing customers using the same product mix?
   - Could new approaches to advertising or promotion persuade customers to increase the size or frequency of their purchases?
   - How could we increase customer loyalty and our share of each customer's purchases?
   - Could prices be adjusted to boost volume and net revenue?
   - Could other existing products or services be cross-sold to current customers of core products?
   - Can we enhance the skills of the salesforce?

2. **New customers.** This involves going to look for new customers either by convincing the ones of your competitors or by being innovative and looking elsewhere, where there are unexploited markets.
   - How could we extend the business by selling existing products to new customers?
   - Could new approaches to advertising and promotion capture new customers in existing segments?
   - Are there entirely new customer segments that might be interested in existing products and services?
   - How can these products or services be repositioned for these new segments?
   - Are there partnerships or alliances we could form to increase the reach of existing products and services?
   - Could we bundle these products and services in ways that appeal to new customers?

3. **New products and services.** This involves developing new products and services to accommodate the needs of your existing customer base or indeed of an entirely new one.
   - How could we grow by introducing new products and services?
   - What extensions or modifications to existing products and services would fill gaps in our market coverage?
   - What customer need is our current product or service satisfying, and what is the ideal product or service for that need?
   - What fundamentally new products or services could be developed to cater for emerging or latent demand?
   - Are there any products or product lines that can be purchased or licensed to complement our current range?

4. **New delivery approaches.** This focuses on examining if there are different routes to market and different ways that the product and services could reach the final customer.
   - How could we expand sales by developing better delivery systems for customers?
   - What marketing channels still have to be explored (direct sales, electronic channels, new distributors)?
   - Are there substitute channels for existing products?
   - Is a direct channel now feasible?
   - Can the business delivery system be reengineered to improve time, cost, and quality?

5. **New geographic areas.** This deals with the possibility of entering new geographic areas not yet targeted by the firm.
   - How and where could we expand into new geographical areas?
   - Are there opportunities to extend points of distribution in existing territories?
   - Are there opportunities to enter underserved regions within the boundaries of an existing national business?

- Could production cost or quality advantages be exploited via exports?
- Could global coverage drive economies of scale?
- In which new markets could our business model be exploited?

6. **New industry structure.** This focuses on the possibility of changing the structure of the industry either by integrating vertically or horizontally.
   - How much could we grow by changing the industry structure through acquisitions or alliances?
   - Which troubled industry participants could be acquired at the right price and turned around?
   - Which parts of the industry could be consolidated via acquisitions?
   - Are there economies of scale or other competitive advantages in doing so?

7. **New competitive arenas.** The final level deals with the opportunity of creating new untapped market 'blue oceans' where competition will not exist.
   - What opportunities are there outside existing industry boundaries?
   - Are there opportunities to integrate vertically and create competitive advantages?
   - Could our business skills be used in other industries?
   - Do we have unique assets that could be used to create new businesses?
   - Could any of our relationships be used to gain access to new businesses?
   - Are other industries converging on our industry?

Selecting the best potential solutions

You may by now have a long list of potential solutions. But it is probably not a good idea to try them all. If you do, you are likely to be spreading your energy and resources too thinly. You also need to understand which ideas could have the most impact and how much effort they will take to implement. At this stage, it is important to make trade-offs to enable you to focus on the initiatives that will bring you the best return on the resources you invest. But how can you decide which solution to pursue and which ones to leave? The impact/effort grid is a useful tool for comparing the likely costs and benefits of each solution. For each potential course of action, the grid requires you to estimate both the likely impact and the amount of effort it will require.

The assessment of the likely impact should be geared at understanding how much of the core challenge the solution might solve. This assessment does not necessarily have to be directly driven by financial considerations. For instance, if a core challenge is to instil in the company a culture of implementation (getting things done), any solution that drastically improves the lead time of projects and the mind-set of people might be a good candidate.

The assessment of the effort must take into account the available resources such as people, skills, technology and finance. Something that might be complex and demanding for one company to implement might be relatively simple for another.

You may have to use guestimates rather than exact figures, but this will not invalidate the process. Having done this for each of the choices you are considering, you can now make comparisons and start ranking the options in terms of their overall desirability. Looking at the case of energy cost reduction that we examined using a logic tree, should we focus on (a) improving isolation, (b) use new primary sources of energy, or (c) optimise our own versus independent power generators? Or, alternatively, should we (d) optimise the regulating systems? Perhaps a combination of (a) and (c) would create the best short-term results, while not being too difficult to implement. Whereas optimising the regulating systems (d) might bring better long-term results but would be more complex to achieve.

Using the impact/effort grid to filter your options will help remove some of the risk from the process. We have not made any irreversible choices as yet. We are still at the stage of assumptions and hypotheses. Testing these hypotheses will tell us if we are on the right track to solve our core challenge and help us avoid any dead-ends.

Figure 8.5 shows a priority matrix with potential solutions evaluated according to the effort they would require and the impact they may have on overcoming the core challenge. The upper-right square is clearly where there is a need to focus. However, you may need to work on solution 5 which might have a substantial impact in the medium term. If the company is in need of cash, solution 3 might also be worth considering. It will have limited impact but requires little effort.

Timing initiatives

Another important element to consider is when to implement the retained strategic initiatives. We often hear managers say that a certain idea is pointless because it would take too long to implement and the company needs quick results. As a result, lots of potentially valuable ideas are discarded because too much attention is paid to the immediate future. But a company that over-focuses on the short term does not have much of a long-term future. Instead, when thinking about implementing initiatives, companies need to have in mind three different horizons.

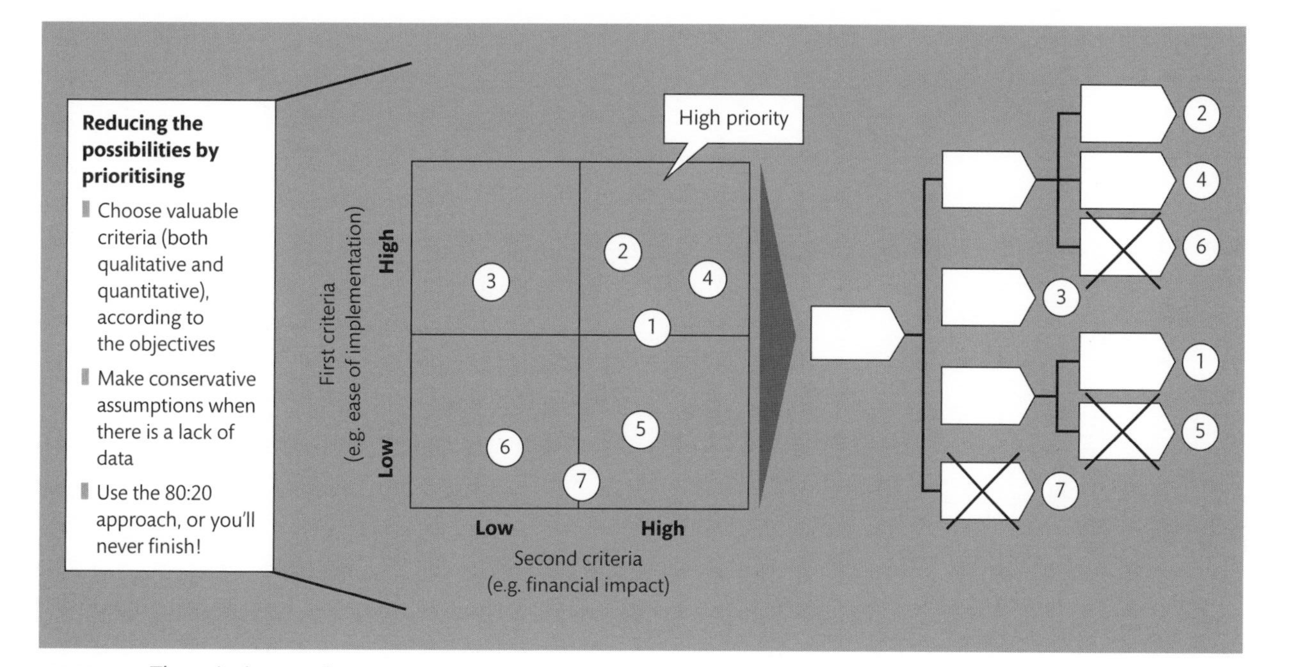

FIGURE 8.5 The priority matrix

Source: based on McKinsey principles

Horizon 1 encompasses the businesses that are at the heart of an organisation – those that customers and stock analysts most readily identify with the corporate name. In successful companies, these businesses usually account for the lion's share of profits and cash flow. Horizon 1 businesses are critical to near-term performance, and the cash they generate and the skills they nurture provide resources for growth. They usually have some growth potential left, but will eventually flatten out and decline. Even when these are mature, continuous innovation can incrementally extend their growth and profitability.

Traditional salesforce stimulation programmes, product extensions, and marketing changes can all contribute. Restructuring, productivity enhancement, and cost reduction measures will also help maintain healthy performance for as long as possible.

Horizon 2 comprises businesses on the rise: fast-moving, entrepreneurial ventures in which a concept is taking root or growth is accelerating. The emerging stars of the company, these businesses are attracting investors' attention. They could transform their company, but not without considerable investment. Though substantial profits may be four or five years away, they have customers and revenue, and may already generate some profit. More importantly, they are expected to become as profitable as horizon 1 businesses in time.

Horizon 2 initiatives are usually characterised by a single-minded drive to increase revenue and market share. They need continuing investment to finance roll-outs or otherwise accelerate the expansion of the business. In a few years, horizon 2 initiatives should complement or replace a company's current core business. They may represent either extensions of these businesses or moves in new directions that might substantially affect the current business model.

Horizon 3 contains the seeds of tomorrow's businesses – options on future opportunities. Although embryonic, horizon 3 options are more than ideas. They are the research projects, test-market pilots, alliances, minority stakes, and memoranda of understanding that mark the first steps towards actual businesses, even though they may not produce profits for a decade, if ever. Should they prove successful, they will be expected to reach horizon 1 levels of profitability.

A company that thinks it has a promising horizon 3 just because it compiles a long list of whiteboard ideas at a management retreat is fooling itself. Without deliberate initiatives to develop good ideas into horizon 3 opportunities, a company's long-term growth prospects will fade. The options in horizon 3 are rarely proven opportunities, but they need to be promising and to have the support of management. Building successful businesses means seeding numerous options. Some will fail for internal reasons; others will fall victim to shifting industry winds. Most will never grow to become successful new businesses. Given these odds, a great deal of horizon 3 activity is needed to cover the multitude of possible futures. A company goal should be to keep the option to play without committing too much capital or other resources. The challenge is to nurture promising options while ruthlessly excising those with diminishing potential.

Keeping all three horizons in mind will help a company to think in a more balanced and circumspect way about the nature, focus and timing of its new initiatives. Although the right amount of attention to give to each horizon will inevitably vary according to context, a recommended focus (in terms of time, energy and money) would go along the lines of 70% for horizon 1, 20–25% for horizon 2 and 5–10% for horizon 3.

Through using the three-horizon framework companies should be able to avoid having a portfolio of products or services that is unsustainable.

As a company looks at the spread of its initiatives across the three horizons, there are four patterns that should raise a 'red flag' because they indicate weak overall growth prospects (see Figure 8.6):

1. **Losing the right to grow** – companies that focus on growth so much that they neglect their core businesses may lose the right to grow as their fundamental profitability becomes threatened.
2. **Running out of steam** – companies that focus too much on operational excellence and do not look to future growth are threatened with extinction if their core businesses mature and nothing is available to fuel future growth.
3. **Generating ideas but not building businesses** – companies that focus on horizon 3 type options, but fail to generate horizon 2 growth engines run the risk of not having enough momentum to exercise those options when their current growth engines mature.
4. **Failing to sow seeds for the future** – companies that develop the next phase of growth, but do not sow the seeds of options for a further phase, are also threatened by decline as horizon 2 withers over time due a lack of horizon 3 options developing.

When devising strategic initiatives, it is then important to balance their implementation over the three horizons, as shown in Figure 8.7. For each horizon, it is also useful to define how performance will be measured and the core skills that will be needed.

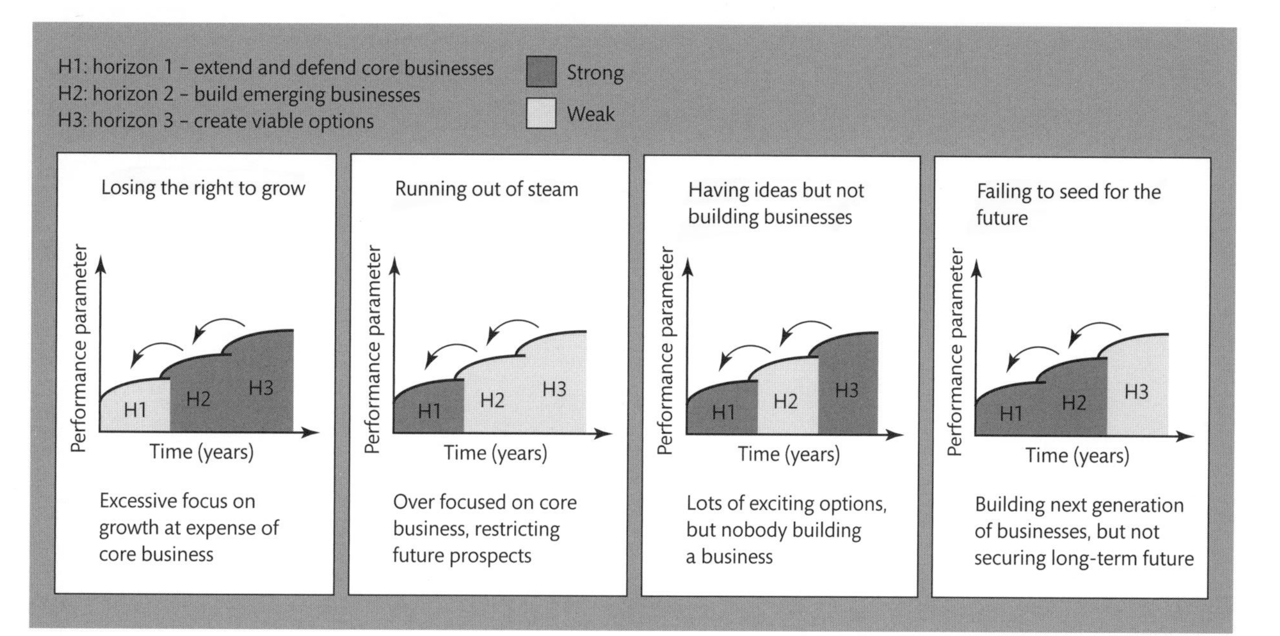

FIGURE 8.6 Pitfalls of the three horizons

Source: based on Baghai, M. , Coley, S. and White, D. (2000) *The Alchemy of Growth: Practical Insights for Building the Enduring Enterprise*, Perseus Books Group

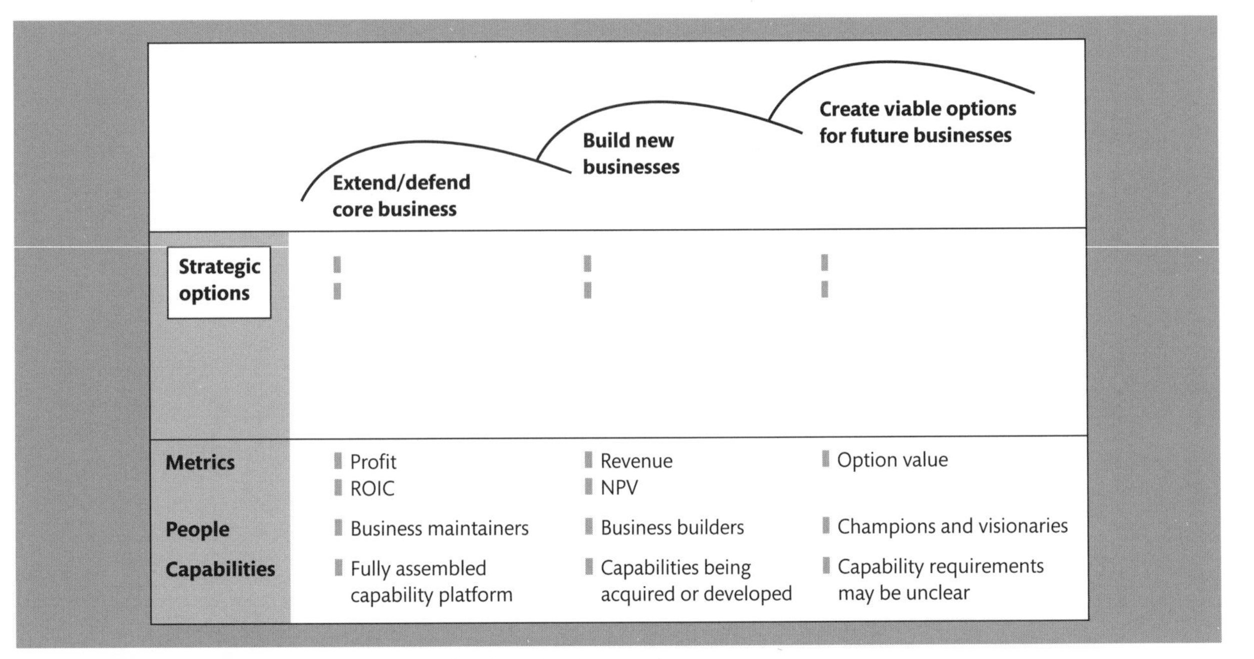

FIGURE 8.7 Plotting strategic initiatives on the three horizons

Source: based on Baghai, M., Coley, S. and White, D. (2000) *The Alchemy of Growth: Practical Insights for Building the Enduring Enterprise*, Perseus Books Group

The key messages of this chapter

- Core challenges are not easy to solve by nature (otherwise they would not be core challenges). The first step in tackling a core challenge is therefore to reduce its complexity.
- This can be achieved by breaking down the core challenge into a number of simpler components (the constituents). To this end, logic trees obeying the rule of relevance, coherence and MECEness can be used. Mind mapping is another useful technique.
- Logic trees and mind maps are helpful in simplifying the issue, but lateral thinking that triggers intuition and imagination will get you nearer to a solution. Tools and techniques such as solution-shop approach, co-creation workshops, blue ocean strategy or the seven degrees of freedom will help you find potential solutions.
- Lateral thinking might enable you to come up with a long list of potential solutions. But it is probably unwise to try them all. You might be spreading your energy and resources too thinly. Using a priority matrix is helpful in understanding which ideas could have the most impact and how much effort they will take to implement.
- Last but not least, it is key to time the implementation of the potential solutions. Not all should and can be started right now. Focus the effort on what brings immediate results but do not forget the rest.

ACTION POINTS

- Simplify your core challenges by breaking them down into simpler problems, using the power of logic trees and mind maps to understand which key constituents need to be tackled first and are a necessary route to finding a solution to the core challenge.

- Think widely, differently and laterally. Do not get discouraged by the common 'we've tried that before', 'this will never work', or 'that's too farfetched'. Many successful companies started from crazy ideas! Leverage existing frameworks such as the blue ocean strategy or the seven degrees of freedom to stimulate the development of creative, yet simple solutions.
- Use an impact/effort grid and make guesstimates to select the best potential solutions you need to focus on, so you can address your core challenge effectively.
- Time your solutions or strategic initiatives with a three-horizon framework.

9 Reducing uncertainty

ABOUT A YEAR AGO Davide was having a discussion with a former classmate who is now a top executive at a telecoms company. We were talking about the strategic challenges that his firm was facing and how they could figure out how to deal with them. As he talked, it was clear that he had put a lot of thought and energy in the development of a sound strategy, but it was evident that something was bothering him. In spite of having worked out a way forward, he still seemed agitated. When I asked him about this, he replied, 'Davide, the biggest problem I have is how to manage the uncertainty linked to the strategy. I know that the solutions and the initiatives we have found are good, but I also know that some will not work or not deliver the impact expected, or worse not deliver it in the timeframe we have set. We have planned for the short term with some initiatives that will have an impact within the next six months, but I still need to make the investment and then wait for the impact. It's the same for the mid- and long-term initiatives with the downside that the wait will be much longer and the investment much bigger.'

These concerns are typical of any top manager who has been involved in strategy development. You may have spent a lot of time and resources identifying and then selecting the best available options, but until you implement them you cannot be sure that they will deliver the desired outcome.

Uncertainty in strategy has many facets. First, there is uncertainty around value creation and whether the identified actions will deliver benefits that outweigh the effort involved. Second, there is uncertainty about the potential for increasing the scale of the initiative. In some cases, actions either cannot be scaled up or when they are, the level of returns diminishes rapidly. Last but not least there can be uncertainty regarding the sustainability of the actions the organisation has chosen to implement.

There are two main factors at work in this aspect of uncertainty, one external and the other internal. Externally, the easier it is for competitors to imitate and therefore cancel out the advantage flowing from an initiative, the less sustainable it will be. Internally, the issue is how well the strategy will be received and adopted by the organisation. Even if the strategy is well researched and conceptually sound, if it conflicts with the culture of the organisation the invisible hand will be working against it, erecting barriers which may be insurmountable.

The previous chapter outlined a number of ways of identifying potential solutions to our core challenge. But as practical as the frameworks and tools we have offered can be, we are still in the realm of hypothesis, where there is no guarantee that our potential solutions will work when tested in the real world. Finding the solution to a core challenge is not something we can achieve in a single event. Instead, it is likely to be a step-by-step process where we test out our assumptions before moving forward another step. This process of testing and learning and gradually refining our thinking is essential if we are to find robust answers.

This chapter is dedicated to reviewing how executives can reduce the level of uncertainty around the strategy and the initiatives that they have developed. We will first look at the role of experimentation and how this approach can substantially reduce the amount of risk associated with a strategy even before it is launched. Then we will outline ways of tracking and monitoring the progress of the initiatives that passed the experimentation phase and that you have chosen to implement, as they take shape in the real world.

Experimenting to reduce uncertainty

Chapter 8 showed a number of techniques that will help you to identify strategic initiatives for overcoming core challenges. Any such initiatives rely on a set of hypotheses. A hypothesis, in business as in science, is an explanation or a proposition made on the basis of limited evidence as the starting point for further investigation. Until proven true, hypotheses are just statements. The only way to prove their validity is to test them. Testing will either prove or disprove the validity of a hypothesis, but it will also provide insights about how the hypothesis could be refined or even replaced by a better one.

Just like a scientist, executives should first make explicit the hypotheses behind their initiatives and then validate them through experiments. A practical and iterative approach, called **lean testing**, allows executives to quickly and inexpensively test out the hypothesis behind a potential strategic initiative. Lean testing has four phases that need to be performed in the correct sequence (see Figure 9.1). As you move from each phase to the next, the overall level of uncertainty reduces. But it is not until the initiative has passed all four phases that it should be put forward for full implementation.

Lean testing, like any testing methodology, requires a disciplined, well-managed process and a good knowledge of the tools and techniques that can be used. To use lean testing successfully, you need to be clear about which tests will be

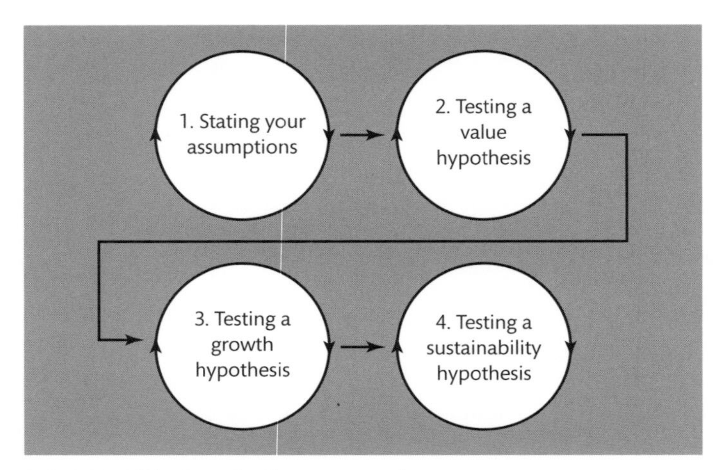

FIGURE 9.1 The lean testing approach

carried out, in which order, and the metrics you will use to judge the outcome and decide whether or not the hypothesis has been proved. Many testing tools and techniques are available (see below) and new ones can always be developed. However, the most important thing is to select the ones that are the most appropriate for your particular circumstances.

The fitness for purpose of any technique will depend on the time and resources you have available, but the ideal should be something which is simple, quick and inexpensive. Unfortunately, this ideal is sometimes forgotten and companies often use incredibly sophisticated statistical techniques when a much simpler approach based on average, median and variance would have been more than sufficient.

Before getting into the detail of how to perform lean testing, a note of caution. Some people mistakenly think that lean testing is the same as running a pilot phase. It is in fact entirely different.

Phase 1: Stating the underlying assumptions

This first phase does two things. It helps to uncover any potential design flaws in the initiative even before we run any tests, and it also clarifies the elements to be tested in the subsequent three phases.

Stating the underlying assumptions involves not only describing how the initiative will solve a particular problem but also making explicit the assumptions that underpin the thinking behind the initiative. These may be assumptions about staff performance, customer preference, economic trends or any aspect of the internal or external environment. But no matter how reasonable they may seem or how much they reflect current thinking in the industry, they must be made explicit.

Many management proposals rest on assumptions that are never mentioned, usually because we tend to be unaware of the assumptions we are making. But every unexamined assumption represents a hostage to fortune, something that may prove difficult or even fatal later in the process.

The process starts by categorising the underlying assumptions along three dimensions: value, growth and sustainability. For each of these dimensions there is a set of questions to be addressed which will highlight potential design flaws.

The first dimension is **value**, which involves explaining how the initiative will create value by producing outcomes that outweigh the effort involved. The typical questions that need to be addressed are:

- What kind of problem does the initiative solve?
- Who are the people facing this problem? How aware are they of the problem?

- Are they prepared to pay for someone to solve it?
- Will the price they are prepared to pay for the solution be sufficient to cover the cost of its production?

The second dimension is **growth**. Here we must think through how the initiative can be scaled up beyond the first group of pioneering customers, guaranteeing that the value created will also increase sufficiently. The typical questions to be addressed are:

- Does the solution address the needs of a large enough group of people?
- Will the initiative need to be changed or adapted for this enlarged group?
- How difficult and how costly would it be to scale up to meet increased demand?
- What is needed for the initiative to appeal to this larger group?
- Will the price need to be changed?
- How could we reach and engage a growing group of users? How much would this cost?
- Will the increase in users be reflected in increasing value creation, i.e. will the increase in outcomes outstrip the increase of the cost of achieving such growth?

The last dimension is **sustainability** which has two mutually reinforcing facets. The first relates to the ease with which competitors can replicate the initiative and the second concerns how easily the organisation itself will accept the changes required to implement the initiative. The typical questions for the first facet are:

- How easily can the competition imitate the initiative or substitute it with another product? How long would it take?

- What kind of barriers are there which will preserve the advantage?
- Are there other barriers we could create? How much would they cost?

And for the second facet:

- How will the organisation need to change to enable the initiative to be implemented?
- Will the organisation be able to cope with such changes?
- Is there something about the initiative that we can adapt in order to make it more acceptable to the people and culture of the organisation? What impact would this adaptation have in terms of value creation?

By addressing these questions you will be able to decide whether the initiative merits being moved forward. Furthermore, this approach will help you to identify potentially serious flaws which require fixing before the initiative can be progressed

In the following pages we will describe a number of concepts that are essential in ensuring the effectiveness of lean testing. These include: MVP/MVS, smokescreen testing, Fishbone analysis, A/B testing, and cohort analysis.

Minimum viable product or service (MVP orMVS)

A **MVP or MVS**, as the name suggests, is a cost-efficient way of testing just a few features of a new product or service. A MVP or MVS contains only those features that need to be tested against the dimensions of value, growth and sustainability.

A MVP/MVS is progressive in the sense that several versions will be built with each new version incorporating the learning gained from the previous ones. The learning at each stage supplies insights on how to adapt the MVP/MVS based on the feedback received from potential users. Starting with the pioneers and early adopters who are very willing to buy into a new product and share their feedback, the MVP/MVS is introduced to different groups of customers.

As the MVP process moves on, other types of users are introduced, including more sceptical ones who will provide new insights into how the product's features could be improved but also into how best to communicate with customers. This aspect of customer feedback is as important as comments about the product itself, since the failure to communicate its benefits is a common reason for a product failing to break through into the mainstream.

This approach improves the chances of success by exploring how acceptable a new idea is to its target audience before large amounts of time and money have been committed. For example Zappos, the shoe retailer bought by Amazon, was created through a progressive evolution of MVPs starting with a very basic website which offered many different types of shoes for sale, despite the fact that Zappos had no shoes in stock. When a customer placed an order, the founders would run to a shoe shop, buy the shoes (sometimes at a loss), then package them and send them to the online customer. They used this MVP to test, quickly and cheaply, their value hypothesis: i.e. that some people would be prepared to buy shoes online.

Phase 2: Testing assumptions about value

Testing the assumptions about value requires us to address a number of questions, starting with the most basic one; whether there is a problem worth solving, and whether someone will be prepared to pay for a solution. We call this the customer problem hypothesis. Being wrong about the customer problem hypothesis is the worst thing that can happen. You would end up with a product, a service or a strategy that does not correspond to the needs of the customers and, consequently, has no value for them.

To test the customer problem hypothesis, use a very simple approach that combines:

- a fishbone analysis to establish what type of benefits would be seen as a good solution by different audiences; and
- a smokescreen test that emphasises the features of the potential new solution as opposed to existing solutions. Different versions may be needed for different types of audience.

The smokescreen is presented to a sample of potential customers in order to test and refine your customer problem hypothesis. The main outcomes should be a confirmation that customers are prepared to pay for a solution and an indication of the group of customers which has the most 'vivid' need: i.e. the customers keenest to have access to the solution.

Another important activity to perform during this second phase is an initial, high-level assessment of the cost of assembling and delivering the product or service. Of course the cost, once the initiative is up and running, has to be lower than the price the customer is prepared to pay. But this does not mean that you must be able to make a profit during this phase of testing. Indeed, having a cost that is higher than the price is normal at this stage since the learning curve will be steep and economies of scale are not yet applicable. Nevertheless, it should be possible to develop a realistic target cost to compare with the likely price. Only when the relationship between cost and price guarantees value creation should you move to the next phase.

Smokescreen testing

The **smokescreen test** is the simplest type of MVP/MVS. It is a description of the product or service you want to test, perhaps backed up with some marketing material such as a brochure or basic website. It is an ideal way of finding out if there are people with a problem or a need which your product will address and whether they are prepared to pay for the solution you offer.

We worked on a project to offer a sophisticated data analysis service to healthcare organisations. A foundational assumption that we needed to test was that these organisations would be prepared to purchase such a service. Until this hypothesis was proved, it would be foolish to pour large amounts of resource into the project. So, we produced a high-quality brochure and put together an attractive spreadsheet that showed the sort of statistical analysis we could provide. We then organised meetings with physicians and managers, the people who could make decisions about purchasing services, and used our brochures and spreadsheets to illustrate what was on offer. As well as confirming that there was a need to be met, these discussions provided us with valuable ideas about how to refine the product, which otherwise would not have occurred to us.

Using a smokescreen test before assembling a more highly developed MVP/MVS is a cost-efficient way of gauging customer response and reducing risk.

Fishbone analysis

Fishbone analysis is a tried and tested way of identifying the potential causes of a problem. It is all the more effective because it is a highly visual method and can be used as the focus of a group discussion. The problem to be addressed is the 'head' of the fish and the main bones radiating out from the spine are the categories or types of causes that could be considered in the search for what is causing the problem (see Figure 9.2). Depending on the context, these categories might include people, equipment, policies, systems or materials. After deciding on the main categories, the group brainstorms possible causes within each category and attaches these to the main bones. A fishbone analysis is a good way to visualise ways of checking if a problem is worth solving.

For example, a new online feature of a business-to-business website could simultaneously:

- improve the time to deal with customer complaints (providing online guidance) that customer service would welcome;

- prompt an alert to an account manager that there may be an opportunity for new business (upgrade of an existing system) with an existing customer, which would be welcomed by the business development department.

If such a feature is tested using the same type of communication to both audiences this may have a very different outcome if the testing was differentiated, emphasising the most relevant features to the relevant group.

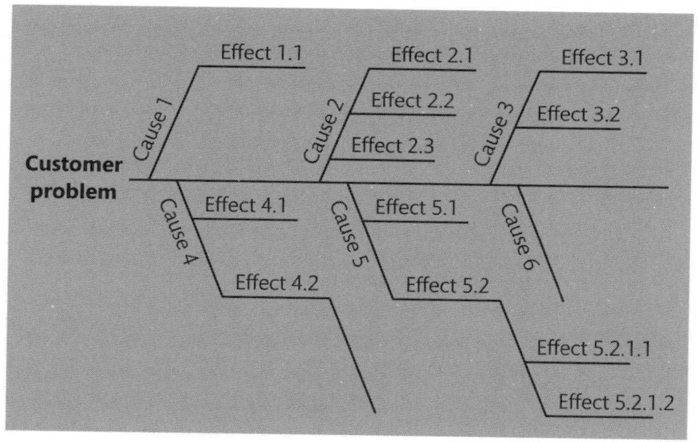

FIGURE 9.2 Fishbone analysis

Source: based on Ishikawa, K. (1968) *Guide to Quality Control*, Asian Productivity Organisation

Phase 3: Testing assumptions about growth

Once we have established that there are some customers who have a problem that they would like to solve, and that we have a solution that these customers would be willing to spend money on, the next question is: how can we profitably reach a large enough group of customers? It is crucial to ensure that a demand exists from a large enough customer base and that we have an effective growth engine – a way of reaching and adding more customers.

Organisations sometimes come up with products or internal projects which will only appeal to a very small number of people. Unless this is a deliberate and considered move, as in some luxury sectors, the product cannot create much value. Or sometimes the cost of reaching a larger group is so high that it wipes out most of the value created.

There are three main types of growth engine:

1. **Viral engine of growth.** Here the engine of growth is the customers who find the product or service so valuable that they become ambassadors, promoting it to other potential customers. This growth engine is normally very cost effective, although it would be wrong to believe that it comes completely free. Often organisations need to put in place resources, tools and processes to allow such engines to operate at maximum speed. Word of mouth is the oldest viral engine of growth. When a product or service delivers much more than the expected value, then people are eager to share it with others, triggering the viral engine of growth.
2. **Paid engine of growth.** This involves paying for the acquisition of new customers. This can take many different forms such as investing in communication (e.g. advertising), in incentives (e.g. discounts or bonuses) or in new product features (e.g. different formats, styles or colours). It is worth pursuing this strategy of growth only when the cost of growth is less than the increase in profit.
3. **'Sticky' engine of growth.** This engine operates in parallel to, and in support of, the previous ones. It works by retaining as many customers as possible and ensuring that they do not stop using the product or switch to an alternative. Customer loyalty is the key, so that they 'stick' with your product. This can be achieved through viral techniques or through investment.

Investing in an engine of growth is very costly in terms of cash and energy so we need to make sure that we choose the right way of growing the audience for our product. This is particularly important because we often fall victim to what many call **vanity metrics**. Vanity metrics are mental biases that our mind creates to justify our desire to pursue a particular solution when in reality it is not worth the investment.

Imagine that we have launched a new product and that we have introduced it to 1000 customers of whom 50 (5%) responded positively. Building on this early success we promote the product to a second group of customers and this time we get 40 customers out of 1000 to buy it. Encouraged by this, we take it to another 1000 customers and this time 20 of them decide to buy. The vanity metric would be to measure the numerical increase in customers which went from 50 to 110, a growth of 120%, whereas a more objective approach would be to highlight the worrying reduction in the sales conversion rate which dropped from 5% to 2%.

To select an engine of growth, there are a number of techniques that can be used, in particular **A/B testing** and **cohort analysis**. These will help to quickly test many different options drawn from the four Ps of marketing (product features, pricing, promotion and placement) and their impact in terms of profitable growth, in order to select the combination that will yield the highest return. An engine of growth may have a limited lifespan in terms of its effectiveness. So we many need to use more than one engine, and by tracking and comparing the performance of the different engines we can ensure that we are investing in the right ones.

A/B testing

A/B Testing (often referred to as split testing) is a simple experimental methodology to test which of two alternative features is the more productive. An example of this might be an advertising campaign which puts a percentage discount (e.g. 20%) in front of one group of customers and a cash discount (e.g. £5) in front of another. This approach could be used to test and compare two potential alternative features of a MVP/MVS, helping to identify the target audience's preference.

We would then use the results of the A/B test to decide which features to incorporate into the product for the next version of the MVP/MVS.

Cohort analysis

Cohort analysis involves the study of different parameters and activities of a cohort (a group of people who share a common characteristic over a certain period of time). For example, we can form customer cohorts based on their same joining data and perform a cohort analysis on their purchasing patterns (e.g. frequency, value) over a period of time. When multiple cohorts are tested, comparisons between them can be used to identify key business parameters such as ideal introductory offer, customer journey, promotion frequency, etc.

Cohort analysis used in conjunction with A/B testing could be used to assess the effectiveness of different combinations of product features, communication messages, pricing and distribution channels.

Phase 4: Testing assumptions about sustainability

You have now reached a point where you have sound reasons for believing that your proposed solution can create value and that there is a large enough group of potential users who can be reached to enable benefits to keep growing in proportion to costs. Building on the learning gained from the previous three phases, in this next phase you will be testing ways of enhancing the sustainability of your solution.

Sustainability is the result of two mutually reinforcing factors. The first of these is the ease with which competitors can replicate your initiative. The second is how easily the organisation itself will accept the changes required to implement the initiative. The more difficult your solution is to copy and the more adaptable your organisation is, the longer you will be able to sustain value.

Initiatives that have proven to be valuable and scalable will be very appealing to the competition. They will naturally attempt to replicate these initiatives in order to seize a share of the benefits. So it is important to consider ways of slowing down or even preventing this replication and test them out to gauge their effectiveness.

Here are three approaches that companies have used successfully but do not let these limit your creativity. Use your imagination to develop and test new ones.

1. **Adding features to create a 'black box'.** Initiatives composed of several interrelated elements are much more difficult to replicate than ones with just one or two elements. Even if none of the elements, taken individually, are hard to copy, their combination and the way in which they work together will be difficult for competitors to figure out and replicate, creating a sort of black box.
2. **Intellectual property protection.** Particularly for new and innovative products or services, it may be possible to obtain intellectual property protection. This ranges from simply trademarking the brand to applying for a patent. Although taking a rival to court should be

considered as a last resort, the simple fact of having intellectual property protection will make other businesses think carefully before they try to reproduce your product.

3. **Customer or supplier lock-in.** Another good way of increasing the difficulty for competitors to replicate the initiative and take a share of the value is to use contracts and partnership agreements that encourage long-term, exclusive relationships between the company and its customers and suppliers.

The second factor that determines sustainability is the ability, and willingness, of your organisation to flex its systems, resources and ways of working to accommodate the new product or service. Company culture plays a large part in this, as the 'invisible hand' either smooths the path to change or puts up barriers. It is possible to have, on paper, everything needed for implementing the new initiative but to fail because of the attitudes and mind-sets of employees. There are a number of things that can be done to reduce the risk that the organisation will reject a new initiative, and we will explore these in depth in the next chapter.

Testing sustainability is hard to do without involving a significant number of customers and a large part of the organisation, and this phase represents a halfway point or bridge between lean testing and the full roll-out. For this reason, sustainability starts with a partial roll-out. This needs to be done in a planned and controlled way. We call this a progressive roll-out.

As the name suggests, this approach starts with a limited number of customers or users and gradually increases this number towards full roll-out. Facebook famously uses progressive roll-out when it releases new features on its website, starting with 1000 users, then 10,000, 100,000, 1,000,000 and so on until every member is reached. The obvious advantage of the progressive roll-out is that it enables lessons to be learned before the number of customers affected is too great. Responding to 1000 complaints is better than trying to cope with millions of unhappy customers. It is also worth noting that some problems only become visible as usage increases, and a controlled, progressive roll-out enables these issues to be identified and fixed at the earliest possible stage.

Ongoing testing and learning

There are two good ways of carrying the testing mind-set forward into the implementation phase:

The programme office

The **programme office**, often referred to as the project management office (PMO), is a team whose task is to monitor the progress of initiatives and to intervene when the outcomes differ from the objectives. There are no established rules about membership and composition of a PMO team. Best practice organisations tend to create a core team with dedicated full-time staff who bring different skills and perspectives and who can access other skills as and when required. Normally, the PMO reports directly to the board or CEO.

Using a PMO approach increases success as measured by a project's key performance indicators of quality, scope, schedule, budgets and benefits. This is confirmed by surveys of organisations that excel in project execution, which show that operating an established PMO is one of the main drivers of successful project delivery.

The strategic-thinking process tests potential solutions to core challenges and learns from this process, in order to either change direction or proceed to roll-out. The PMO plays a critical role in checking, as the initiatives are rolled out, the accuracy of the assumptions about value, growth and sustainability. It makes sense of the learning gained from real-life experience and converts it, on-the-go, into continuous improvement. The PMO team focuses not only on monitoring but also, and more importantly, on learning, as it gathers feedback and uses it to improve outcomes.

A PMO also facilitates the right conditions for open and constructive dialogue in the organisation. Most innovative companies acknowledge the importance of corporate dialogue by arguing that regular meetings between managers, or between managers and employees, should be part of the performance measurement system. An effective dialogue system, composed of regular meetings, enables the exchange of knowledge and shared experiences among individuals and contributes to reinforcing the organisational culture and strategy. Creating the right structure for performance meetings that encourage creative dialogue will turn information into a powerful resource for competitive advantage. A PMO can provide a helpful setting for constructive dialogue about initiatives and what can be learned from them.

The Rexam example

Rexam, a world leader in the production of aluminium cans, launched a major programme when it faced a significant lack of efficiency across its European plants. This core challenge was tackled with a series of solutions to improve throughput, reduce waste and improve delivery. The need for urgent improvement and tangible results was such that the company decided to launch the implementation of all solutions (after a successful testing phase) simultaneously in 15 plants across Europe.

In order to closely monitor the evolution of the pilots, a PMO was set up, with daily conference calls to help manage and stabilise the implementation. During these calls, in which all plants participated, ideas were exchanged and experiences were shared. The focus was not on control or punishment but rather on the rapid dissemination of best practices and accelerating the learning process. As the process unfolded it emerged that some plants were leading in certain areas while others had the edge in different areas. The PMO helped lessons learned in one plant to be quickly assimilated elsewhere.

The control tower

The concept of a **control tower** or **war room** has its origin in the command centres used in military or government contexts to centralise the oversight of a campaign. A war room enables all the main aspects of an operation to be monitored and managed in real time. Like an air traffic control centre that monitors and directs the movement of aircraft, a war room allows organisations to view the current status of important initiatives. In this respect, war rooms could also be described as control towers.

War rooms can be seen as a set of carefully chosen indicators that help managers make swift and well-informed decisions, instead of having to painstakingly gather together data from a variety of sources. When rolling out an initiative after a successful testing phase, it is essential to keep a very close eye on progress. Keep in mind that implementation, even if it is well thought through, takes place in a context of high uncertainty. Constantly checking the expected outcomes against reality is the only way to avoid dangerous deviations. The earlier a deviation from the plan is spotted, the easier it is to take corrective action.

We recently supported a field force engaged in a cross-selling initiative. We provided the force with documents giving advice on which products should be offered to which types of customer, which lines of argument could be used and even how to calculate the potential for cross-selling. Within a few days after launch, we could see that the first results were not living up to our expectations. Feedback from the sales team made it clear that our supporting documents were too complex for them to use in front of a customer. This was something that had not been picked up on during the prelaunch lean testing. What had been helpful for the enthusiastic members of the sales force who had participated in the testing phase was not effective during the general roll-out when all sales staff were asked to use the new documentation. The early warning provided by the control tower enabled us to redesign the documents in conjunction with sales staff.

Cellfish Media's bit of bling

When Cellfish Media, the US leading mobile content provider, decided to launch its mobile brand BlingTones – a series of innovative applications, games, ringtones and wallpapers, the company first piloted the launch of a few samples to test the market. Cellfish closely followed the take-up rate of a variety of samples, correlating them with customer profiles. It also tracked indicators such as response rates to test messages sent to users who had shown an initial interest. This allowed for real-time fine tuning of the offer, dynamically adjusting the nature of content being offered to specific customer groups.

The team also followed the evolution of sales, tracking down frequency and time of purchase, size of basket, types of content and evidence of diffusion through social networks. All of this helped minimise risk and encourage success in a crowded and highly uncertain market where social media could instantly make any product an immediate hit or a definitive failure.

The key messages of this chapter

- Uncertainty in strategy has many facets. First, there is uncertainty around value creation and whether the identified actions will deliver benefits that outweigh the effort involved. Second, there is uncertainty about the potential for increasing the scale of the initiative. Finally there can be uncertainty regarding the sustainability of the actions the organisation has chosen to implement.

- There are two main factors at work in this aspect of uncertainty, one external and the other internal. Externally, the easier it is for competitors to imitate and therefore cancel out the advantage flowing from an initiative, the less sustainable it will be. Internally, the issue is how well the strategy will be received and adopted by the organisation.
- A practical and iterative approach, lean testing, allows executives to quickly and inexpensively test out the hypothesis behind a potential strategic initiative. Lean testing has four phases: stating the underlying assumptions, testing assumptions about value, testing assumptions about growth, and testing assumptions about sustainability.
- After the testing phase, the testing mind-set should be carried forward and implemented through the programme office and the control tower.
- The programme office (or PMO) is a team whose task is to monitor the progress of initiatives and to intervene when the outcomes differ from the objectives.
- The concept of a control tower (or war room) has its origin in the command centres used in military or government contexts to centralise the oversight of a campaign. A control tower enables all the main aspects of an operation to be monitored and managed in real time.

ACTION POINTS

- State your assumptions behind your suggested solution. Write down what should be true for the solution to yield the desired outcome. Structure the assumption along three dimensions: value, growth and sustainability.
- Think how you could test the features of your solutions in the most inexpensive and rapid way. Design the MVP/MVS

that would constitute a first prototype of the solution, and whose only goal is to test your stated assumptions.

- Introduce your MVP/MVS to the market and perform real testing of your assumptions about value, growth and sustainability. There are useful tools for that as discussed in this chapter.
- Track progress after the testing phase. You could set up a programme office or a control tower that will help you monitor several important milestones and key performance indicators.
- While testing, adjust on the go in line with your learning. Once the test shows full success roll it out as fast as possible. If success does not come after multiple iterations, pivot immediately, and capitalise on the learning.

10 Managing execution

THIS CHAPTER IS DEDICATED TO THE EXECUTION OF STRATEGY. It will help you ensure that the initiatives that you tested and selected to be part of your strategy will actually be implemented and achieve the results you are looking for. In many people's minds, the strategy process ends when the main actions and initiatives have been defined. We have added an extra phase, the one of lean testing. Nevertheless execution must be seen as an integral part of the strategy process and not as a separate standalone activity.

Anyone who has been involved in strategy will know that it is a long, sometimes tortuous, journey. It can be an intricate process involving large numbers of people, all with their own agendas. Most scholars agree that most strategy programmes end in partial or total failure due to organisational issues such as culture, communication and corporate structure. Strategy is about change (so we use *change programme* as a synonym of *strategy execution*) and the truth is that most organisations are not particularly effective at managing change. This chapter's insights will help you join the small percentage of those who can lead change successfully.

Strategy requires a group of people not just to take action, but to take action that is coordinated and complementary. And in our experience, strategy failure can usually be traced back to issues that undermine or prevent this coordination.

Strategy often fails just because people in the organisation do not know *what* their strategy is!

What would be the chance of you meeting your friends at a particular restaurant for dinner tonight if they did not know where they should go or even that you were organising dinner? Obviously, close to zero. Now you may think that this sort of situation could never occur in organisations full of managers with MBAs who are trained in communication and who are masters of PowerPoint. It may seem paradoxical in a business world where we often have too much information rather than too little.

Often when we ask people about their strategy, they have great difficulty in responding with any clarity. They may fall back on telling us their departmental objectives or quote some vague principle from a speech by the CEO. But they do not know what the strategy is and how it impinges on them.

There are two other key reasons for this failure:

1. People do not understand the '*why*' to change: both why the execution of the strategy will lead to a situation that is better than the current one and why (i.e. in which terms) the selected course of actions will contribute to the fulfilment of the organisation's vision. In Chapter 6 we saw that great companies communicate the purpose or belief that drives and animates the entire enterprise. This not only makes them stand out from their more prosaic competitors, but inspires their workforce and makes them feel they are part of something important.

   It is true that people can be told what to do or even forced to act against their will, but such an approach is neither effective nor sustainable. Unless people understand and share the purpose that drives the strategy, the most they can give is compliance. And even this can only work when the actions required are thoroughly explained and will work without any tweaking or adaptation. Only when people have grasped the 'why' behind the strategy will they be motivated and able to successfully adapt and change as circumstances demand – which is the very essence of strategic thinking.

2 Even if people understand the 'what' and 'why', they do not fully understand how they have to change. They do not see a clear link between strategy and practical change. There seems to be a disconnection between strategy and the day-to-day running of the organisation, almost as if strategy happens in a different world and can progress without any changes in the behaviour and activities of employees. In addition, they do not see how their actions should be connected and integrated with others'.

When we encounter this misunderstanding, we ask people to reflect on these three statements:

- **Strategy execution**, defined as the implementation of a set of actions designed to take you from point A to point B, **is about change**.
- **Learning**, defined as the acquisition of new, or the modification of existing behaviour, skills or knowledge, **is about change**.
- Therefore **executing strategy is about learning how to change.**

Strategy execution must be seen as a learning journey. It involves learning about the destination (the what), the path (the how) and reasons for embarking on the journey (the why). It also involves learning about the changes and adaptations that need to happen along the way.

Here you will find out how to avoid, or at least limit the effects of, the factors that lead to failure in strategy execution. First by showing how you can help people act together with purpose and understanding, something we call *shared intentionality*. Then we provide a framework that will support you as you manage and implement your strategy.

A will to act

Two fundamental elements must be in place for successful strategy execution: each and every member of the organisation has to develop a will to act; and these individual intentions must be coordinated in order for the strategic plan to be implemented coherently (coordinated approach).

In Chapter 2 we defined action as purposeful behaviour. Every action is the result of an individual person's thought process which supplies the what, how and why of the action. But in the case of organisational strategy, many different actions need to take place in a coordinated way. Sometimes an action will require the contributions of several people. And because not everything can be planned accurately in advance, many actions will have to be developed from broad guidelines or principles as the strategy execution progresses.

To allow people to cooperate successfully in this way, adapting and improvising as they go, people must be willing to act but their willingness must converge with the strategy objectives. We need to develop a **shared intentionality**: where not only does each person have a will to act but also the intentions of everyone involved are compatible and coordinated.

Humans have a unique ability to think individually while acting collectively and to take account of others' plans and intentions as well as their behaviour. This ability to read and adapt to others' intentions is an important part of our social behaviour and affects many of the decisions we make. Depending on our perception of the intentions of those around us we may change our course of action to, for instance, allow or avoid collaboration. We may also share our intentions with others, hoping that they will modify their behaviour to allow us to achieve our goals.

Shared intentionality can only exist where:

- The individuals concerned have a shared objective. Their reasons for wanting to achieve the objective may differ, but the objective must be shared by all.
- The intentions of the individuals are compatible and interdependent, i.e. the various things the individuals intend to do are mutually reinforcing rather than in conflict.
- Individuals have a clear understanding of each other's intentions.

Shared intentionality in an automotive company

Imagine that a sales executive, a marketing manager, the head of engineering and the head of manufacturing share the goal of launching a new product. Each person may have very different intentions. The sales executive wants to demonstrate her ability to work in a team, the marketing manager wants to boost his promotion prospects by impressing his boss, the head of engineering intends to prove the effectiveness of a new production process and the head of manufacturing needs to show that his department can produce the goods in time. Although different, these intentions are compatible and interdependent. The achievement of any of these intentions will not impede any of the others; in fact success in one will make success in the others more likely. Because of this, the more aware the individuals are of the intentions of their colleagues, the more they will be ready to adapt their own actions to accommodate the others in the team.

A coordinated approach

As we anticipated, converging willingness (shared intentionality) unfortunately is not enough to ensure the successful implementation of the strategy. The other prerequisite is that each and every individual knows how he can contribute with his own actions and that the actions of the different individuals are coordinated within a change programme.

Though a change programme cannot be done through a recipe or a template, it is possible to identify some 'ingredients' and 'best practices' to guide you in establishing a coordinated approach to the implementation. The simple model described below will help guide your actions as you set out on the change journey. It is based on our research and experiences over many years, but we will refer to two companies in particular, an automotive company and an international airline.

The change management model (see Figure 10.1) supports you in the three different phases of the strategy implementation:

1. **Setting the scene** concerns the creation of the **preconditions** that must be in place to allow the change journey to start. Until these are in place there can be no or very limited progress in strategy execution.
2. **Launching and spreading change** concerns the **triggers** of the change programme. In this phase, some elements must be in place in order to create shared intentionality, which is needed for successful change. Without these triggers to spark the process, the other elements are useless.
3. **Accelerating the speed of change** concerns the **boosters** of the change programme. Change can be slow, the boosters will accelerate change by enhancing the impact of the triggers.

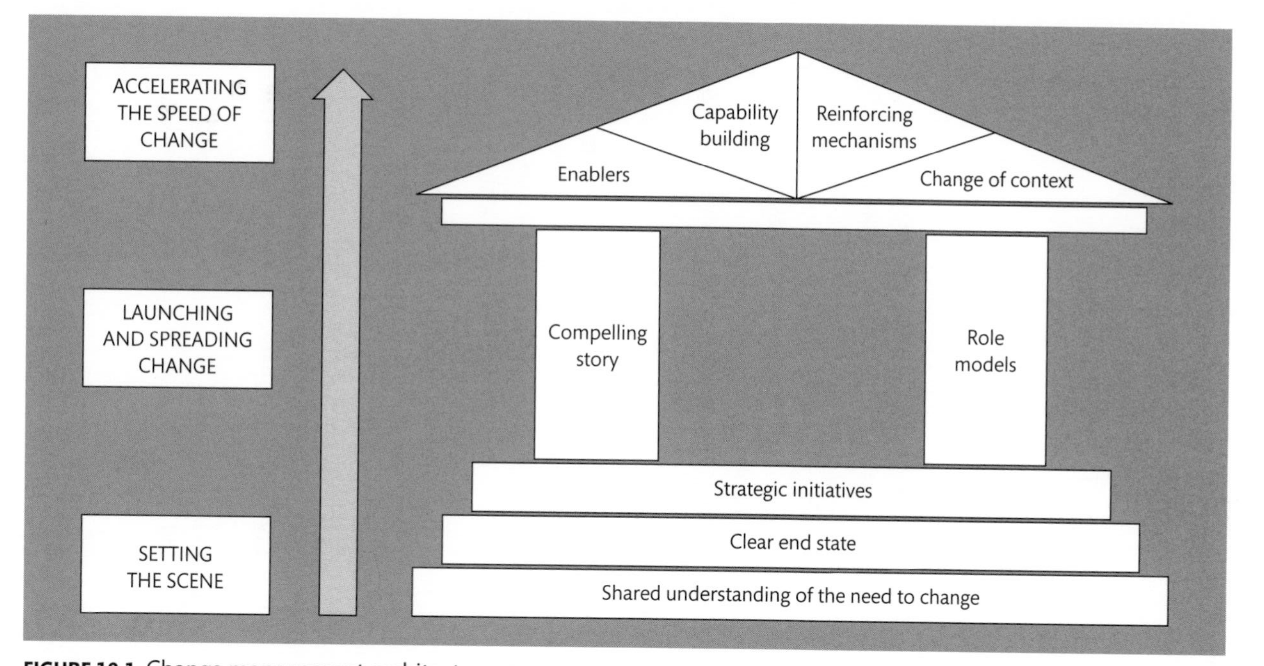

FIGURE 10.1 Change management architecture

Setting the scene

The first element of the model is concerned with creating the right conditions for your organisation to begin a successful change journey. As with the foundations of a house, these conditions are necessary in order to start your building.

The first prerequisite is a **shared understanding that change is necessary** and that action is essential. Many advocate a 'burning platform' approach where a sense of crisis, real or simulated, is used to show that change is a necessity and that maintaining the status quo is not an option. As people are persuaded that the dangers of doing nothing far outweigh any anxieties they may have about change, they more readily embrace the change process. Remember that alongside facts and figures, 'softer' qualitative issues can be persuasive. Being the best, the biggest or the fastest is a motivational pull for many people.

The place of altruistic or moral motivators should also not be ignored. Healthcare professionals will commit to change if they can see that it will lead to tangible benefits for patients. Similarly teachers will often flex and modify their ways of working if they believe it will positively affect children.

The second essential aspect of preparing the ground for change is a **clear end state**. This provides a lucid picture of what the organisation will look like as the result of the changes. But this picture cannot stay just in the minds of the CEO and the senior team, it needs to be shared and owned by all those involved in the changes. The more people can identify with this picture of a desired future state, and the more they feel that they personally have contributed to it, the more effective it will be in creating synergy as the organisation moves forward.

This sense of ownership is much more likely to occur if people are enabled to contribute to the creation or the fleshing out of the picture, rather than just having it launched upon them as a *fait accompli*. A clear end state informs the direction that needs to be taken, the objectives to be achieved and the sort of mind-set and behaviours that will be required. But the description of the end state should be guidelines rather than detailed prescriptions, providing overall direction, not specific solutions.

The third and final prerequisite is defining and communicating the **strategic initiatives associated with the change effort** as well as the more detailed and specific plans that flow from these initiatives. Everyone needs to understand what will be happening and how it will affect them. This helps to align individuals behind the processes and values that will drive the change. Each initiative should clarify:

- the proposed actions;
- the objectives to be achieved – in clear, time-bound and quantifiable terms;
- the person who will sponsor the initiative and those who will be responsible on a day-to-day basis.

As we saw in Chapter 7 a good way of presenting the first two prerequisites – the shared understanding and the clear end state – is the From–To matrix (see Figure 10.2). This helps in visualising and expressing the key guidelines of the change that is required. The first column (From) states the core challenges (problems and opportunities) revealed by the analysis of the situation. These are the priority work areas, the ones that the company needs to focus on. The second column (To) gives an outline of what the strategy aims to achieve in each of the priority work areas. The matrix helpfully outlines the situation the company wants to move from, and where it wants to get to.

The From–To matrix can then be combined with the third prerequisite – the strategic initiatives – to give a succinct

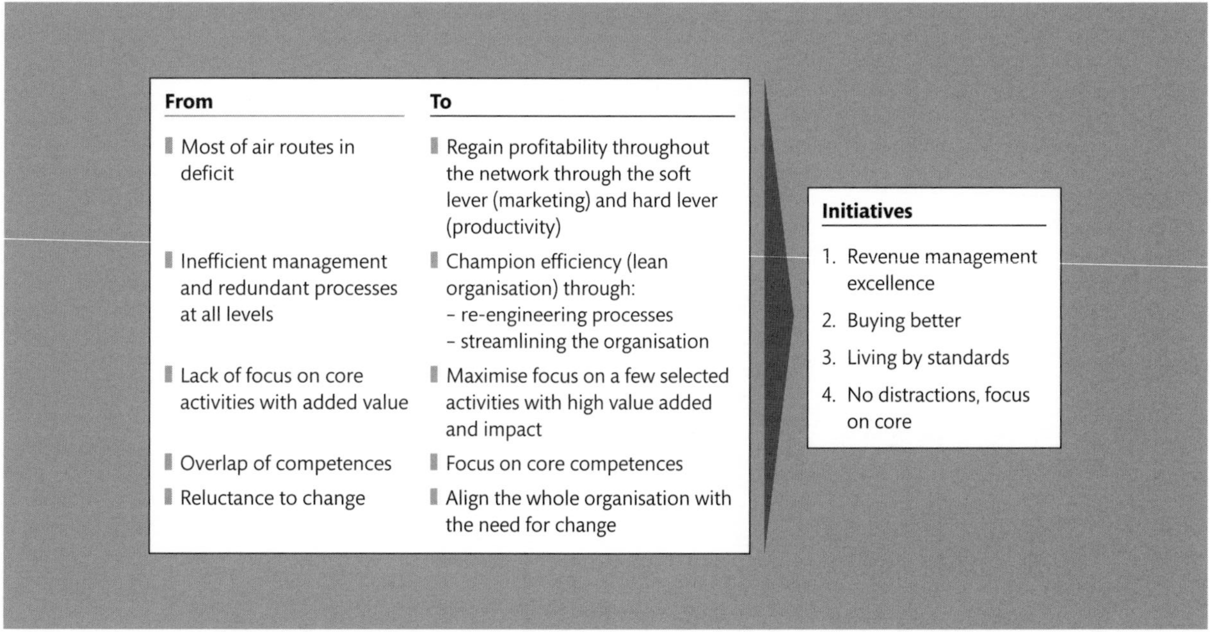

From	To
Most of air routes in deficit	Regain profitability throughout the network through the soft lever (marketing) and hard lever (productivity)
Inefficient management and redundant processes at all levels	Champion efficiency (lean organisation) through: - re-engineering processes - streamlining the organisation
Lack of focus on core activities with added value	Maximise focus on a few selected activities with high value added and impact
Overlap of competences	Focus on core competences
Reluctance to change	Align the whole organisation with the need for change

Initiatives

1. Revenue management excellence
2. Buying better
3. Living by standards
4. No distractions, focus on core

FIGURE 10.2 From–To matrix for an airlines industry player

overview of the what, the how and the why of the strategic change process.

Before we move on from the preconditions for change, here are some important insights gleaned from our experiences with companies going through major change.

Important change insights

- Don't start talking about the pressing need for change unless you can also point the way to a better future. While a sense of threat or danger can be a strong motivating factor, its impact in organisational change is complex and needs to be considered carefully. Communicating that the organisation is in trouble will create high levels of anxiety, and a common response to anxiety is to freeze or stall. Then people are unable to function and may struggle to make even simple decisions. This is not only counter-productive in terms of performance but can also have a profoundly damaging effect on the lives and health of employees as they begin to worry about their livelihood. To avoid this, leaders should bear in mind that they should only communicate about the threats to the company when they can also offer a possible way forward and a vision of the way things will be once the changes are implemented. In other words, don't tell everyone the platform is burning until you can also point to a safe place to jump.
- Keep your list of priorities for change to single figures, ideally no more than five. Too many priorities will diffuse and dilute the energy of the company and you will risk reducing managers to a state of confusion as they wrestle with an impractically long list of things that purport to be absolutely vital. As the saying goes 'when everything is a priority, nothing is a priority'.
- In setting out your priority areas, balance negative with positive. We employ humans, and humans require some hope and encouragement to keep functioning, so if your strategic priorities are all about how bad or weak the company is and how it needs to improve, morale will drop like a stone and any change programme will be weakened before it has started.

As well as highlighting problems, point out areas that are good but could be great and talk about opportunities that can be seized.

- Don't overdo the detail in your strategic initiatives. It's true that people like direction, particularly during periods of change and uncertainty. But when direction becomes prescriptive micro-management the effect will be to squash initiative and kill creativity. The other problem with very detailed plans is that they are a recipe for disaster. They may be based on sound analysis and the best ideas of the brightest minds in the boardroom but because they lack the practical savvy of those who are close to the action, if they are followed to the letter they are likely to lead to failure. Alongside the explicit, written-down knowledge and formal analytical techniques that inform our decisions, companies could not function without the informal know-how that exists at all levels of the organisation. Detailing exactly what must be done leaves no room for adaptation by employees who understand their particular context far better than the CEO ever could.

From–To guidelines for an automotive company

In the case of the automotive company mentioned earlier, it was close to bankruptcy. The new CEO, the fourth in three years, was faced with a company where hope was running out and its morale was as low as its bank balance. Years of poor management, an absence of shared goals and a culture of avoiding the issue had left the company in a desperate state. The new CEO set the scene for change by developing a clear set of From–To guidelines which he called 'how to see the light at the end of the tunnel'. He specified how the culture needed to change and provided a clear vision of where they were going. These guidelines called for a move from technocracy to merit, from authority to leadership, from mediocrity to a continual search for excellence, from being introspective to being competitive, and from vague promises to reliability. To complement these guidelines, there was a set of initiatives that gave practical directions for how to make each From–To journey.

Launching and spreading change

Change leaders generally have two aims in communicating with their teams: to gain their commitment to change and to support them through the painful process of change. They need to persuade, inspire, comfort and urge cooperation.

In launching the change, creating a compelling story and using role modelling are two success factors that every leader embarking on the change journey should leverage.

Creating a compelling story

A communicator seeking to change attitudes has a choice of two main methods: to tell a story or present a well-structured argument. While the skilful use of logic and facts can get the point across, we suggest that when it comes to winning commitment and offering support, narrative may be more effective. Storytelling is a universal and widely accessible form of communication, crossing boundaries of culture and education. Powerful compelling stories not only affect attitudes and ideas, they can have a life of their own as they are repeated and passed on, becoming part of the mythology of an organisation.

Storytelling plays an important role in change by fostering commitment and providing support and encouragement. Stories, in the shape of autobiographies, are popular reading for executives and in many organisations stories about outstanding successes or inspired solutions form part of the culture. When Gordon Shaw, an executive at 3M, looked for a better way to present business plans, he moved away from the usual bullet points approach and began to use stories which, in narrative form, gave a memorable picture of the market, the competition and the strategy needed for success. The result was improved organisational buy-in. According to Shaw, 'When people can locate themselves in the story, their sense of commitment and involvement is enhanced. By conveying a powerful impression of the process of winning, narrative plans can mobilise an entire organisation.'

The success of the story will depend on careful crafting to include the following features:

- The story should be simple enough to be memorable and repeatable.
- It should include examples, objectives and actions that illustrate the change strategy.
- It should be flexible enough for individuals to adapt it to fit their own context and see themselves as part of the story.
- Relevance will draw people into the story and help them see where the company wants to go – the desired end state.
- Describing how challenging and ambitious goals were met, using drama and excitement, will build cohesion and commitment.

The power of storytelling

The power of the compelling story is illustrated by the experience of an international airline that was facing its deepest crisis since the company began in the 1920s. Sales were shrinking and the competition was becoming more and more fierce. Money was being lost at a rate of €2–3 million each day with little prospect of a turnaround. A new CEO was brought in who commissioned a thorough analysis of the company's predicament. Management used the results of this analysis to create a series of stories that fostered a sense of urgency and communicated a picture of how good things could be if the crisis was overcome.

Sub-stories, relating the overall message to each division and department, were also created to help each individual see themselves as part of the journey to success. The mood of excitement tinged with fear of what might happen if changes were not made led to people implementing initiatives that had been talked about before, but never acted on.

> One senior executive said 'In the past, many consultants had explained to me how to leverage elasticity in pricing, but it wasn't till a colleague told me that he could get a 20% premium on standard fares by offering lounge access that I realised why it was so important.' In this case, the colleagues' story of getting an extra 20% brought to life what had previously been only a concept.

Using role models

In your company there will be people who exemplify the sort of thinking and behaviour that are needed to transform the company. It is not just what they say that is helpful but the way they deal with colleagues and clients, and how they approach their work. These are role models. Whether or not they occupy formal leadership positions, these people are leaders in terms of how they are regarded by their colleagues. Because of their standing in the organisation, their behaviour is scrutinised by those around them and sends powerful messages about what is important. They do not influence by email or memo, they 'walk the talk'. They do not just tell a story of how the organisation will move forward, they live it.

There are no recipes for becoming or creating a role model, but they tend to have common attributes. First they demonstrate an understanding of the organisation's people and culture. While they speak they are able to refer to a situation that shows their deep knowledge of people and corporate issues. Second they have a strong presence and public standing. Role models have the confidence and respect of the people around them. They are seen as leaders, either for their technical skills, their managerial competence or their powers of persuasion. People follow their example.

Finally role models are trusted because they 'walk the talk'. The role model embodies, on a day-by-day basis, the compelling story of how the company is moving from its current difficult situation to a better future. Their words and actions communicate and reinforce the values and behaviours that need to be adopted by the whole organisation. They demonstrate real and practical commitment to the company and its strategy.

A role model

In the automotive company, the CEO helped model the change that he wanted to see. Previously in the company, leadership was top-down rather than enabling, with all important decisions being made in the executive suite. In the face of this the CEO stated that, 'My job is not to make decisions about the business but to set stretch objectives and help our managers work out how to reach them. I am the conduit for change, but it's the people in my organisation who actually make change happen.' This was not only a compelling story which signalled a break with the past, but also a true reflection of his behaviour. He would often tell his managers, 'I understand what you are telling me and what you intend to do. You are now in charge, let me know how I can help.' Such readiness to trust and empower had previously been unheard of in the company.

Accelerating the speed of change

The change programme journey often requires a lot of time and effort from the people within the organisation and occasionally moments of discouragement and frustration will be evident. Sustaining change is as important as launching it. People's enthusiasm, commitment and focus should be constantly 'enabled' to boost the change.

In order to accelerate change it is important that the compelling story fast and effectively reaches each and any individual who is expected to contribute. People are reluctant to change if they feel they lack the knowledge, capabilities or skills to give their contribution. So each person must be enabled to perform at his best through adequate training.

Enablers serve as signal boosters, accelerating and widening the transmission of the company's compelling story. In some ways they are similar to role models, being part of the critical mass of engaged and committed people who will bring about transformation. But they have the specific role of accelerating change by using their networks or their professional status. We have identified three types of enablers: connectors, experts and sales people.

Connectors have extensive networks and can use these to spread ideas and information rapidly across the organisation. **Experts** are looked up to by their colleagues because they have exceptional skills and knowledge and are ready to share them with others. Because of this, what they say carries weight. **Sales people** are the persuasive communicators who are able to sell the company's message and who can make even sceptics think again.

Communicating the message depends on having an effective network of enablers. The wider and deeper the network, the quicker the message will spread. It is important to consider the spread of the enabler network in your organisation and to identify areas that may not be reached effectively. Of course, not all enablers are equally effective, but even those whose reach is minimal can act as a gateway to adjacent networks that may otherwise not hear the message.

Speed is of the essence

When the airline set out on its change journey, speed was of the essence. The team leading the change knew they needed to enlist and engage a network of enablers as quickly as possible, but how could they identify the right people to work with? Then one team member suggested emailing everyone in the sales department, asking them to list the people they would normally turn to for help or information. The lists contained the names of people who always seemed to know the answers, the gossip, or the right person to talk to.

> Twelve people were identified and invited to work with the change team and the role models, becoming fully acquainted with the transformation plan. These enablers were then able to reach out to all the sales staff to communicate the vital change message and vouch for the authenticity of the company's intentions, with their personal credibility serving to strengthen the communication.

People generally feel unconformable with abandoning 'trialled and tested' ways of doing things for new ones. Often new ways of doing things require learning new skills. An excellent way to support such transition is capability building.

Capability building programmes can include formal training as well as on-the-job coaching. They need to be based on adult learning techniques that emphasise involvement, discovery and experimentation. If designed well, these programmes will help communicate the new mind-sets, behaviours and knowledge that will facilitate change. They should contain elements of personal and professional development so that staff not only have the new skills, but also the confidence, motivation and initiative to use them.

Designing a capability building programme

- **Focus on the needs of the organisation.** The capabilities and competencies you are aiming to develop must directly address the needs of your organisation as it journeys towards its desired end state.
- **Make it meaningful and relevant for the individual.** The programme must equip people with the skills, knowledge, attitudes and behaviours that they will need to play their part in the change process. It is a golden opportunity to invest in the development of your staff and involve them in the change effort.
- **Use adult learning techniques.** Look beyond just formal classroom teaching. Think about mentoring, coaching, apprenticeships and rotational programmes.

- **Invest time.** Don't skimp on this element of change. The programme needs to be long enough to allow a real, practical enhancement of the capabilities and competences of your employees.
- **Use your role models.** Involve role models in championing the programme. Their credibility and standing within the organisation will rub off on the programmes they are associated with.

Three identified priorities

The airline identified three priorities for its capability building programme: improving sales skills, strengthening management competence and sharpening the company's focus on performance. The change team launched three development initiatives in response to these priorities. They provided tailored training programmes for all staff needing to develop their technical skills, sales skills or managerial competences, and provided coaching for less experienced staff. They complemented these initiatives by recruiting staff who were already well experienced and who would bring fresh energy to the department.

A successful implementation of a change programme means that, even when the sense of urgency and the initial adrenaline has gone, the new behaviours and attitudes are so ingrained in the organisation that they belong to the new 'normality'. In order to 'institutionalise' the new behaviours, as a change leader, you should be able to manage two levers: the change of context and the reinforcing mechanisms.

Every day we repeat many activities in a very familiar environment. An incredibly effective yet inexpensive way of boosting the recognition that change is inevitable and that it will happen is to change the environment (**change of context**). Changes in the physical environment such as new signs, new uniforms or redecoration can help reinforce the message that change is taking hold. These changes have to be visible, meaningful and relevant. **Visible** means that the changes must be noticeable to staff; **meaningful** means the nature of the change must reinforce the change message; and **relevant** means the change must have some impact on people's work or work environment.

Changes in the environment

In both the automotive company and the airline, changes in the environment played a part in accelerating change. The automotive factory area was untidy, poorly lit and in need of a thorough clean. Facilities for the staff were poor and the overall impact on morale was negative. One of the first initiatives launched by the change programme was a refurbishment of the factory, including the provision of childcare and retail facilities close by to help support a healthier work/life balance.

The airline's facilities and equipment had suffered from insufficient investment. The change team saw that some speedy changes in the environment would signal that the intent to change was real. In choosing what to do, their criteria were the amount of effort required for the change and the likely impact on morale and productivity. A new incentive scheme was introduced, sales reporting systems were overhauled and new laptops bought for the sales representatives. As well as bringing tangible benefits, these changes were powerfully symbolic of the company's determination to change.

Finally, **reinforcing mechanisms** are systematic ways of recognising and rewarding employees as they demonstrate the new ways of acting and thinking. For individuals who show that they are embracing change, there are financial or other kinds of reward, but there are also penalties for those who have not yet committed to the journey. These mechanisms must be clearly linked to the direction the company wishes to pursue and given sufficient profile for them to have a symbolic value across the organisation. Reinforcing mechanisms have two main objectives: first to motivate employees to pursue and embrace change and second to confirm the need for change and the company's determination to implement it.

There are typical features found in effective reinforcing mechanisms:

- **Can be positive or negative.** They can be rewards that celebrate the success of an individual or team who have successfully implemented change. As well as financial rewards, companies could use promotions, public recognition or special opportunities for personal development such as a bursary. Alternatively, there could be penalties for those who have not demonstrated the new ways of working.
- **Must be highly visible** within the company in order to have impact. Visible means that they need to have an important grade of exposure so that every member sees the importance of it. The form of exposure depends very much on the organisational culture of the firm. In some it may take the form of a very public and noisy event; in another a much more understated one.
- **Must be clearly linked to the change programme.** This can be achieved using a simple set of key performance indicators (KPIs) which needs to be explained and made transparent, and widely understood by all. It is important that such KPIs are clearly related to the execution of the strategy, helping each person to see where the company stands and how much progress it has achieved.

Rewarding and supporting

In the case of the airline, the change team wanted to develop mechanisms that showed how the company was rewarding and supporting those who were committed to change. Three of the mechanisms they put in place were:

1. a control tower that monitored the progress of every single initiative that had been launched;
2. an incentive and bonus system based on both departmental and individual performance, which meant that departmental targets had to be met before any bonus was paid;
3. a new, structured career planning system, based on clear criteria, that allowed staff to plan and develop their careers within the company. Part of this was the potential for non-performing staff to be dismissed. Because dismissal had been practically unheard of in the past, it was this element that had probably the most impact on employees.

The key messages of this chapter

- Execution is an integral part of the strategy process. It is where assumptions and analysis are tested and provides valuable feedback as to what modifications are needed. Many strategic initiatives end in failure due to organisational factors including culture, communication and corporate structure.
- Failure in strategy is the result of three things: people not knowing what to change, people not knowing how to change and people not knowing why the organisation needs to change.
- Strategy, like learning, is all about change. Successful strategy execution depends on every individual having an intention to act which is coordinated with and complementary to the intentions of others involved in the change – shared intentionality.

- The change management model can be used to achieve shared intentionality. It consists of preconditions that prepare the ground for change, triggers that make change happen and boosters that accelerate the rate of change.
- The preconditions include a shared understanding of the need to change, a vivid picture of where the organisation can be as a result of the changes, and a clear communication of the strategic initiatives associated with the change programme.
- A good way to conceptualise and represent the relationships between the preconditions is a From–To matrix. This shows the priority areas for change (problems and opportunities), the aims of the strategy in relation to each area and the strategic initiatives that will accomplish the changes.
- The triggers that will launch and spread the change include having a compelling story. The presence of respected role models in the organisation, who exemplify the knowledge, skills and behaviours needed to make the change a reality, will also help create shared intentionality.
- To boost the speed and spread of the compelling story, four complementary techniques are recommended: identify and engage enablers; instigate changes in the environment; build capability through training programmes; and have reinforcing mechanisms.

ACTION POINTS

- Think about the need for change in your organisation, the change required to accommodate the suggested solutions. Is there a clear picture of why there is a need for change? Is there another clear picture of what the end state would look like? Get the team together and go through a From–To exercise.

- Define a compelling story that includes why change is needed, how the organisation is moving through change and how it will get there, with specific initiatives. Make sure you make it as simple as possible and communicate with lots of examples, so your people can locate themselves in the story.
- Are you and the leaders behaving like role models! Your team will be looking at you and the way you behave, so walk the talk to be credible. Make sure you embody all the attributes of the change programme. Identify those who could also be role models and try to involve them in the programme.
- Show early signals of change so that all understand that change is now happening! The question is no longer about when the train will leave the station, show that it is about to depart! Early signals can be small in nature but important in significance.
- Try to identify the enablers around you, those who will buy into the need for change and accelerate the diffusion of the change message, respected individuals who will spread the word.
- People might be willing to change but might lack important skills, such as speaking in public, making presentations, using software or acting as leaders. Make sure you get them the right training – this small investment will pay off handsomely!
- Finally, reward, reward, reward those who champion the change programme. Celebrate early and later wins, communicate on success and failures. Be tough and do not reward those who do not want to embrace change.

To discover how to spread strategic thinking throughout your organisation, please download The Strategic Thinking Manifesto for free on **www.howtothinkstrategically.org.**

Glossary: Key concepts and definitions

A/B testing (often referred to as split testing): a simple experimental methodology to test which of two alternative features is the more productive.

Adapting to the fastest: strategy based on the ability to spot and respond quickly to developments, taking the current industry structure as a given and reacting to the opportunities the market offers.

Alignment: the extent to which people within the organisation share similar mental models and a sense of direction.

Blue ocean strategy: an approach based on the view that market boundaries and industry structure are not fixed and that industry players can reconstruct it, not through competition but by creating a new market where there are no competitors.

Business or business unit strategy: a strategy which seeks to establish competitive advantage in each of the company's product or service markets leading to the creation of value in that particular business unit.

Business model analysis: an understanding of what drives the current strategy and how the business system is configured to respond to the demands of the competitive environment.

Co-creation: a relatively new marketing approach which encourages the active involvement of customers in the value chain of the company by integrating their knowledge, experience and creativity in the development of products and services.

Cohort analysis: a study of different parameters and activities of a cohort (a group of people who share a common characteristic over a certain period of time).

Competitive advantage: the result of a strategy capable of helping a firm maintain and sustain a favourable market position. This position is translated into higher profits compared to those obtained by competitors operating in the same industry.

Competitive advantage ecosystem (CAES): a framework which synthesis many different elements, both within and outside the organisation, and their interplay.

Competences: ways in which tangible assets such as machinery or intangible ones such as know-how are deployed.

Concept/idea statement: a clear statement of the assumptions that the solution is based on and the outcomes which would indicate if the solution is correct.

Connectors: enablers that have extensive networks and can use these to spread ideas and information rapidly across the organisation.

Continuous improvement: constantly researching and implementing incremental improvements that will maintain or strengthen your competitive advantage or at least reduce its rate of decay.

Control tower or ***war room:*** a tool which allows organisations to view the current status of important initiatives.

Core competences: activities and processes through which resources are deployed in such a way as to achieve a competitive advantage in ways that others cannot imitate or obtain.

Corporate culture: the deeply embedded belief systems and shared mental models that guide the decisions and actions of an organisation.

Corporate strategy: a plan which addresses the questions of what business the whole company should be in and how the organisation should be managed and structured.

Cost leadership strategy: an approach designed to deliver products or services with features that are acceptable to customers and sold at a price which is in line with the average, but which the organisation is able to produce at a lower relative cost.

Differentiation strategy: an approach that enables a firm to offer products and services that the end customer perceives to be unique, to the point that they are prepared to pay a relative price that is well above the average, while the firm is able to deliver such products and services with a relative cost that is in line with the industry average.

Effect-cause-effect approach: effective way of separating effects from causes and distilling down observations in order to identify a core challenge.

Exiting: the decision to withdraw from the market and redeploy resources elsewhere.

Fishbone analysis: a framework for identifying the potential causes of a problem.

Focus/niche strategy: an approach applying the three value creating options (differentiation, cost leadership and dual strategy) to all segments of a market across geographic boundaries or a focus of effort and energy into a much more selected and limited scope.

From–To framework: a technique that can be used to communicate strategic guidelines, the 'From' represents the core challenges and the 'To' is the desired outcome that will result from overcoming them.

Functional strategy: a strategy which addresses questions specific to the functions of the company.

Governance and organisational structure: roles, responsibilities and decision-making powers, relationships and interactions, and channels of communication between the different stakeholders.

Internal shocks: sudden change of leadership or any event that leaves its mark on the firm.

Invisible hand: self-regulating behaviour of markets.

Lean testing: finding out if the assumptions made in reaching a solution will stand up in the real world.

Logic trees: graphical breakdown of an issue into its various components.

MECEness: characteristic of logic trees, according to which the branches must be mutually exclusive and collectively exhaustive.

Mental models: mental representations of the world around us and how it works.

Minimum viable product or service (MVP or MVS): cost-efficient way of testing just a few features of a new product or service against the dimensions of value, growth and sustainability.

Mission: organisation's reason, the purpose why it exists.

Organisational culture: DNA of the organisation, which is the company's deeply embedded belief system and shared mental models.

Organisation belief system: a collection of mental models that are shared by its members.

Organisational values: principles that guide the behaviour of people in the organisation.

Paid engine of growth: paying for the acquisition of new customers such as investing in communication (e.g. advertising), in incentives (e.g. discounts or bonuses) or in new product features (e.g. different formats, styles or colours).

Performance dialogue: a series of meetings which positively benchmarks different practices within the organisation.

Porter's five forces model: a framework for studying the forces at work within an industry and their interplay.

Profit pools: different levels of profit available in different parts of the value network.

Programme office: team whose task is to monitor the progress of initiatives and to intervene when the outcomes differ from the objectives.

Relative cost: cost of a product or service compared to the average cost of others in the same market.

Relative price: price of a company's product or service in relation to the market average.

Reserving the right to play: non-committal posture, and is sometimes a response to situations currently in a state of uncertainty but which may offer opportunities at some point in the future.

Resources: key production factors, both tangible and intangible.

Return on invested capital (ROIC): a measure which weights the profits a company generates versus all the funds invested in it, operating expenses and capital.

Seven degrees of freedom: a framework for generating potential solutions, adapted to core challenges of topline growth, when a steep and sustainable increase of sales is needed.

Shared intentionality: the ability and motivation to act in a collaborative and cooperative way with joint goals and intentions.

Smokescreen test: description of the product or service to test, perhaps backed up with marketing material.

'Sticky' engine of growth: retaining as many customers as possible and ensuring that they do not stop using the product or switch to an alternative.

Strategic objectives: one or few specific metrics and targets, defined for each core challenge.

Strategy: set of coordinated, creative and sustainable actions (a plan) designed to overcome one or more core challenges that create value.

Structural sources of competitive advantage: resources or assets which an organisation owns or controls and which cannot be accessed or copied by competitors.

SWOT: an analysis classifying the results of the situation analysis into strengths and weakness (from business model analysis) and opportunity and threats (from external analysis).

Three horizons: a framework for managing current performance while maximising future opportunities for growth.

TOWS matrix: a tool to establish correlations and identify potential core challenges by building on the SWOT and applying the company's identified strengths and weaknesses to the threats and opportunities present in the external environment.

Value: positive difference between the outcome of any action and the effort of performing it.

Value chain model: framework for understanding how value is created or lost in terms of the activities undertaken by the organisation.

Value network: set of inter-organisational links and relationships that are necessary to create a product or a service.

Value proposition: the sum of the benefits that the organisation promises to deliver to its customers, through its offering, for which those customers are willing to pay.

Vanity metrics: mental biases that our mind creates to justify our desire to pursue a particular solution when in reality it is not worth the investment.

Viral engine of growth: customers who find the product or service so valuable that they become ambassadors, promoting it to other potential customers.

Vision: envisioned future, a loose description of how the world would be better if certain challenges are overcome.

Sources and further reading

Chapter 1

Chandler, A. D., Jr. (1962) *Strategy and Structure: Chapters in the History of the American Industrial Enterprise*, MIT Press.

Hamel, G. (1998) 'Strategy Innovation and Quest for Value', *Sloan Management Review*, Winter, p. 3.

Mintzberg, H. (1987) 'Crafting Strategy', *Harvard Business Review*, July/August.

Orwell, G. (2000) *Animal Farm*, Penguin Classics.

Porter, M. E. (1980) *Competitive Strategy*, Free Press.

Sun Tzu translated and annotated by R. L. Wing (1988) *The Art of War*, Main Street Books.

Chapter 2

Chabris, C. F. and Simons, D. J. (2010) *The Invisible Gorilla: and other ways our intuition deceives us*, Crown Publishers.

de Bono, E. (1985) *Six Thinking Hats*, Little, Brown and Company.

Goleman, D. P. (1995) *Emotional Intelligence: Why it can matter more than IQ for character, health and lifelong achievement*, Bantam Books.

Kahneman, D. (2012) *Thinking, Fast and Slow*, Penguin.

Loehle, G. (1996) *Thinking Strategically*, Cambridge University Press.

Chapter 3

Drucker, P. F. (2006) *The Practice of Management*, HarperBusiness.

Isaacs, W. N. (1993) 'Taking Flight: Dialogue, Collective Thinking, and Organizational Learning', http://wayra. nl/wp-content/uploads/2012/07/Dialogue-Collective-Thinking-and-Org-Learning_WilliamIsaacs_MIT_1993. pdf (Accessed 11 May 2013).

Peters, T. J. and Waterman, R. H. (1982) *In Search of Excellence – Lessons from America's Best-Run Companies*, HarperCollins Publishers.

Revans, R. W. (1998) *ABC of Action Learning*, Lemos and Crane.

Schon, D. A. (1991) *The Reflective Practitioner: How professionals think in action*, Basic Books.

Sloan, J. (2006) *Learning to Think Strategically*, Elsevier.

Chapter 4

Box, T. M. and Byus, K. (2005) 'Ryanair (2005) Successful Low Cost Leadership', Allied Academies International Conference, Proceedings of the International Academy for Case Studies, Vol. 12, No. 2.

Porter, M. E. (1980) *Competitive Strategy*, Free Press.

Chapter 5

Carney, M. (2012) 'For Tony Hsieh, Zappos' Success Has Been All About Culture and Control', http://pandodaily.com/2012/09/13/for-tony-hsieh-zappos-success-has-been-all-about-culture-and-control/ (Accessed March 2013).

Courtney, H., Kirkland, J. and Viguerie, P. (1997) 'Strategy Under Uncertainty', *Harvard Business Review*, Vol. 75, Issue 6.

De Vries, J. V. (2010) 'Is Leo Apotheker a Good Fit as HPs New CEO?', http://blogs. wsj. com/digits/2010/09/30/is-leo-apotheker-a-good-fit-as-h-ps-new-ceo/ (Accessed March 2013).

Frei, F. and Morriss, A. (2012) 'Now Multiply It All by Culture', *How to Win by Putting Customers at the Core of Your Business*, Harvard Business Review Press.

Hardy, Q. (2010) 'What Leo Apotheker, HPs New Chief, Must Do', Forbes Staff, http://www. forbes. com/sites/ quentinhardy/2010/09/30/what-hps-new-chief-must-do/ (Accessed March 2013).

Heathfield, S. M. (2013) '20 Ways Zappos Reinforces Its Company Culture', Human Resources, http://humanresources. about.com/od/organizationalculture/a/how-zappos-reinforces-its-company-culture.htm (Accessed March 2013).

Hurwitz, J. (2011) 'Can HP Change its DNA?', Harvard Business Review Blog Network, http://blogs. hbr.org/cs/2011/10/can_ hp_change_its_dna. html (Accessed March 2013).

Knowledge @ Wharton (2010) 'Can HP's New Leadership Create a Vision for the Future?', http://knowledge.wharton. upenn.edu/article.cfm?articleid=2620 (Accessed March 2013).

Louis, T. (2012) 'Below the Surface', *Business Insider*, http:// www.tnl.net/blog/2012/06/23/below-the-surface/#sthash. d908jQGJ.dpbs (Accessed March 2013).

Malby, B. (2006) *How Does Leadership Make a Difference to Organisational Culture and Effectiveness?*, Northern Leadership Academy.

Meehan, P., Rigby, D. and Rogers, P. (2008) 'Creating and Sustaining a Winning Culture', *Harvard Management Update*, Vol. 13, Issue 1.

Merchant, N. (2011) 'Why Culture Always Trumps Strategy', *Business Insider*, http://articles. businessinsider. com/2011-03-25/strategy/29991660_1_culture-glues-team (Accessed March 2013).

Owen, K., Mundy, R., Guild, W. and Guild, R. (2001) 'Creating and Sustaining the High Performance Organization', *Managing Service Quality*, Vol. 11, No. 1, pp. 10–21.

Rainey, D. (2010) 'Amateurs Talk Strategy, Superstars Concentrate on Culture', http://www.businessinsider.com/

culture-determines-the-winner-not-strategy-or-tactics-2010–12 (Accessed March 2013).

Rush, J. (2011) 'Culture and Why it Matters to Your Business', *Cross Cultural Strategies*, http://www.crossculturalstrategies.com/2011/02/28/culture-and-why-it-matters-to-your-business/ (Accessed March 2013).

Schein E. S. (1990) *Organizational Culture*, Sloan School of Management, Massachusetts Institute of Technology.

Shukla, V. (2011) 'Relationship Between Organizational Culture & Business Strategy', http://www.brighthub.com/office/human-resources/articles/115483.aspx (Accessed March 2013).

Sims, P. (2011) 'As Hewlett Packard Goes, So Goes the World', Media Files, http://blogs.reuters.com/mediafile/2011/09/28/as-hewlett-packard-goes-so-goes-the-world/ (Accessed March 2013).

Smith, A. (1786) 'An Inquiry Into the Nature and Causes of the Wealth of Nations', Cosimo Classics.

Sole, D. and Wilson, D. G. (2002) 'Storytelling in Organizations: The power and traps of using stories to share knowledge in organizations', Harvard Graduate School of Education.

Song, X. (2009) 'Why do Change Management Strategies Fail?', *Journal of Cambridge Studies*, Vol. 4. No.1.

Tharp, B. M. (2009) *Diagnosing Organizational Culture*, Howarth.

Chapter 6

Christensen, C. M. (2009) 'Clay Christensen's Milkshake Marketing', Innovation Summits, http://hbswk. hbs.edu/item/6496.html (Accessed March 2013).

Christensen, C. M., Anthony, S. D., Berstell, G. and Nitterhouse, D. (2007) 'Finding the Right Job For Your Products', http://sloanreview.mit.edu/article/finding-the-right-job-for-your-product/ (Accessed April 2013).

Dadj, N. (2011) 'Media Convergence and Business Ecosystems', *Global Media Journal*, Vol. 11, No. 19.

Johnson, G. and Whittington, R. (2009) *Fundamentals of Strategy*, Pearson Education.

Levine, R. (2011) 'How the internet has all but destroyed the market for films, music and newspapers', *The Guardian*, http://www.guardian.co.uk/media/2011/aug/14/robert-levine-digital-free-ride (Accessed April 2013).

Magretta, J. (2011) *Understanding Michael Porter: The Essential Guide to Competition and Strategy*, Harvard Business Press Books.

Nobel, C. (2012) 'Empathy, segmentation, and jobs-to-be-done theory', http://blog. rjowen.me/post/29563232468/empathy-segmentation-and-jobs-to-be-done-theory (Accessed April 2013).

Oestreicher, K. (2009) 'Segmentation & The Jobs-To-Be-Done Theory: A conceptual approach to explaining product failure', Sixteenth Annual South Dakota International Business Conference, Rapid City, South Dakota , USA, http://eprints.worc.ac.uk/701/1/Segmentation%26JTBD_Theory_CEIB.pdf (Accessed April 2013).

Porter, M. (1980) *Competitive Strategy: Techniques for analysing industries and competitors*, Free Press.

Porter, M. (1985) '*Competitive Advantage: Creating and sustaining superior performance*', Free Press.

Porter, M. (2008) 'The Five Competitive Forces That Shape Strategy', *Harvard Business Review*, Vol. 86, Issue 1.

Prahalad, C. K. and Hamel, G. (1990) 'The Core Competence of the Corporation,' *Harvard Business Review*, May–June.

Press, G. (2012) 'What Has Steve Jobs Wrought?', *Forbes*, http://www.forbes.com/sites/gilpress/2012/10/10/what-has-steve-jobs-wrought/ (Accessed April 2013).

Ulwick, T. (2013) 'What Jobs Will Apple's Television Get Done?' Business and Product Strategy Blog, http://strategyn.com/2013/01/22/what-jobs-will-apples-television-get-done/ (Accessed April 2013).

Walton, N. and Oestreicher, K. (2011) 'Google & Apple's Gale of Creative Destruction', working paper, Eurasia Business and

Economics Society (EBES) 2011 conference, http://eprints.worc.ac.uk/1348/1/Google_and_Apple's_Gale_of_Creative_Destruction. pdf (Accessed April 2013).

Watanabe, M. (2006) *Your Value Proposition: The foundation of strategy*, BenchMark Consulting International .

Chapters 7 and 8

Baghai, M., Coley, S. and White D. (2000) *The Alchemy of Growth: Practical insights for building the enduring enterprise*, Perseus Books Group.

Chan, K. W. and Mauborgne R. (2005) *Blue Ocean Strategy: How to create uncontested market space and make competition irrelevant*, Harvard Business Press.

Christensen, C. M., Grossman, J. H. and Hwan, J. (2008) *The Innovator's Prescription: A Disruptive Solution for Health Care*, McGraw-Hill.

De Bono, E. (1990) *Lateral Thinking: Creativity step by step*, Harper Colophon.

Prahalad, C. K. and Ramaswamy, V. (2004) *The Future of Competition: Co-Creating unique value with customers*, Harvard Business Review Press.

Rasiel, E. M. (1999) *The McKinsey Way: Using the techniques of the world's top strategic consultants to help you and your business*, McGraw-Hill.

Chapter 9

Blank, S. G. (2005) *The Four Steps to the Epiphany*, Quad/Graphics.

Ishikawa, K. (1968) *Guide to Quality Control*, Tokyo.

Ries, E. (2011) *The Lean Startup: How today's entrepreneurs use continuous innovation to create radically successful businesses*, Crown Business.

Chapter 10

Bratman, M. E. (1999) *Faces of Intention*, Cambridge University Press.

Sola D., Taillard M. and Scarso-Borioli G. (2010) 'Orchestrating Change: Shared intentions is the key factor enabling change to happen', in Verma, S. (ed.), *Towards the Next Orbit, Corporate Odyssey*, Sage, pp. 245–266.

Tomasello, M. and Carpenter, M. (2007) 'Shared Intentionality', *Developmental Science*, Vol. 10, No. 1, pp. 121–125.

Tomasello, M., Carpenter, M., Call, J., Behne, T. and Moll, H. (2005) 'Understanding and Sharing Intentions: The origins of cultural cognition', *Behavioral and Brain Sciences*, Vol. 28, No. 5.

Index